Begin Your Biz in 15 Minutes/Day:

Your Freelancing Tips Starter Kit

by
Sagan Morrow

Copyright © 2018 by Sagan Morrow

All rights reserved. This book or any portion thereof may not be reproduced or used in any manner whatsoever without the express written permission of the author, except for the use of brief quotations in a book review.

Book Designed by Acepub

Contents

Introduction 1

Chapter 1: Step-by-Step Freelancing Starter Kit 5

Chapter 2: Prioritizing Your Business 9

Chapter 3: Goal-Setting & Big-Picture
Business Planning 11

Chapter 4: Create Your Business Plan 19

Chapter 5: Create an Ideal Client
Profile & Prospect Directory 25

Chapter 6: Create a Marketing Plan 31

Chapter 7: Improve Your Website 37

Chapter 8: Pitch Prospects 43

Chapter 9: Client Retention Strategies 51

Chapter 10: Automate & Streamline
Your Business 57

Chapter 11: Confidence-Boosting Strategies 63

Chapter 12: Launch a New Product/
Service/Offer 69

Chapter 13: Manage Your Time Effectively 75

Chapter 14: Reduce Overwhelm in Business 81

Chapter 15: Next Steps 87

Chapter 16: Additional Resources 89

About the Author 91

Introduction

I've been a blogger and freelancer since 2008. It wasn't always an easy path, and at various points I was freelancing full-time and part-time, until I quit my 9 to 5 job for good in 2014.

Then, in 2016, I began teaching other freelancers how they, too, could start and grow their own successful, profitable freelance businesses. I did this primarily through my blog and e-courses at SaganMorrow.com. Over the course of the last few years, I've had the great privilege to connect with hundreds of other new and struggling freelancers, and hear their stories and experiences.

Without fail, two of the biggest issues that frustrate freelancers the most are a) finding the time to begin and build their business, and b) feeling overwhelmed by all the things they "should" do or "need" to do, to the point that many have no idea at all what to work on and what not to work on.

It's with that in mind that I created the (free) Begin Your Biz Challenge: a Facebook group with new prompts every day, sharing action steps you can take to further your business in just 15 minutes at a time.

Totally doable, right? Right!

It gets better: with the Begin Your Biz Challenge, I arrange each of the daily 15-minute action steps to correspond to a specific monthly theme. That way, community members can work together to make progress in specific areas of their business... whether that means creating a business plan one month, identifying their ideal client the next month, pitching new clients the following month, improving their websites the next month, and so on and so forth.

But, here's the thing: it's easy to forget about a Facebook group. It's easy to lose track of the daily prompts and fall behind. And for those people joining the group a little late to the party, it seems like a shame for them to miss out on valuable past monthly themes.

And *that* is why I decided to write this book. So that you can access some of the most popular monthly themes from the past, and take the opportunity to make real progress on your business, in just 15 minutes each day...

Because you're busy. Your life is hectic. Maybe your business is a side hustle, maybe you're taking care of kids or aging parents, maybe you're dealing with mental health issues, or something else entirely.

That's okay. You really can make progress on your business in just 15 minutes/day! Every step, no matter how small, counts. It's not a race to the finish. It's a journey, and one that you can enjoy—especially when you reduce overwhelm by knowing exactly what to work on, when.

And that's what you're going to get from this book.

How to use this book

Chapter 1 outlines the basic steps you need to take in order to start a freelance business. Chapter 2 provides some reminders about why prioritizing your business is so important. From there, Chapters 3–14 each outline 30 action steps to take regarding that chapter topic. Consider it to be your monthly "theme" for the Begin Your Biz Challenge.

I recommend you do the chapters in order, which would then provide you with an entire year's worth of daily 15-minute action steps for your business! (And it doesn't have to start on January 1st: you do you. Why not get started today?)

Note that every single chapter, or monthly theme, includes "catch up on tasks" days, as well as opportunities to plan ahead for the month, assess your business progress to date, and reflect back on the previous month. Some action steps are also more about doing research and learning something new, rather than producing a specific result. That's because all of those pieces are necessary in order to move forward successfully with your freelance business.

This book wraps up with Chapter 15, which suggests where to go from here, and Chapter 16, which includes a list of all the resources mentioned in this book so you can easily access them in one place.

At some point with your business, you'll want to devote more than 15 minutes/day to it in order to make faster progress. That doesn't have to be a week from now or six months from now—but if you're serious about being a freelancer, then somewhere down the line you'll need to accommodate more time for it in your day. I'm gently reminding you of this now so that you can start tentatively thinking about when you might be able to spend more time on your business (it's okay if that's a year from now or even longer): you don't want it to come as a nasty shock abruptly down the line, after all.

*Be sure to get the fillable checklists that correspond with every single chapter at **SaganMorrow.com/beginbook!***

Want to be a rebel when using this book?

You can of course do more than one action step per day if you prefer. Just keep in mind that this is all about bite-sized actions to reduce overwhelm and keep you on track with your business! If you try to do too many tasks in one day, you might start to feel burned out. Take care of yourself, take it one step at a time, and you will get there, my friend.

Sagan Morrow

Chapter 1

Step-by-Step Freelancing Starter Kit

If you picked up this book, you're probably a brand-new freelancer. With that in mind, we're going to start at the very beginning with what you need to do to begin your business, step-by-step.

Psst... have you already started your freelance business, but you still want a little help along the way? Cool! In that case, skip ahead to Chapter 2.

We'll go over each one of these steps in further detail throughout this book, but for now, we're simply looking at the broad strokes of what needs to be done to start a business from the ground-up.

Here's what you need to do when you're starting your freelance business:

Step 1: Decide what type of business you'll have & what services you'll offer.

For example, if you want to be a freelance writer, what type of writing do you want to do for clients? What could those services look like? In this instance, if you wanted to write about health and wellness, would you be more interested in writing blog posts for healthy living websites, research articles for magazines, marketing copy for a non-profit in the health industry...?

As you can see, there are many different types of services and packages you could offer within that broader category. Figuring this out will enable you to be much more intentional and strategic about your marketing so that you'll be able to find the perfect gigs for you, that much faster.

Step 2: Identify who your ideal client is.

Knowing who you are trying to reach is an extremely important step to take, before you actually do any marketing for your business whatsoever. Think of it this way: if you don't know who you're marketing to... then how on earth are you supposed to figure out where they spend their time, what kinds of messaging they'll best respond to, or the rates they can afford?

I know how tempting it is to skip this step, but it's crucial to save yourself a whole lot of time, energy, and frustration. Your future self will thank you.

Step 3: Put together your business plan.

At this stage, you're outlining your mission statement and values, goals, services (and pricing model), budget, financial projections, sick-day plan, etc.

Your business plan should be an organic, living document that steers the ship of your business. Have fun with it! It will change as you and your business grow and change. It doesn't have to be a scary or daunting task: nothing in your business plan is set in stone.

Step 4: Create a marketing strategy.

Here, you can consider which social media platforms you'll need to create accounts for, do an assessment of your website (or if you don't have one, look into getting one set up), determine what in-person networking options there are, and schedule marketing into your daily and/or weekly plan of action.

Step 5: Identify what tools you need for your business.

This is where you'll want to find a great accountant (they are worth their weight in gold! If you spend money *anywhere* in your business, it should be on an accountant. They'll be able to help you out with all those things that are specific to your unique situation, given the type of business you have and where you're located on the globe).

Other tools I highly recommend are things like bookkeeping software (I adore Zoho), a time-tracking app (Toggl is my favourite), and a social media scheduler (MeetEdgar is wonderful).

Step 6: Market your business and find clients.

Yes: once you have the foundations of your business set up, you'll have to eventually put yourself out there to market your business and pitch yourself so you get hired! This is one of the aspects about business that most freelancers get especially nervous about, but it really doesn't need to be as scary as you think. In fact, the way I like to do it is to focus on building real, meaningful relationships so that marketing feels organic (and so that you won't have to be remotely salesy or sleazy).

Step 7: Pivot and stay organized.

This is kind of a bonus step: once you have the foundations in place by doing the above six steps, your business will be well underway... but you could get overwhelmed or off-track easily if your business isn't maintained and organized to keep moving forward and to grow and evolve as you do.

That's why, in this book you'll see that we go far beyond the act of getting clients (which is fundamental—after all, if you don't have clients then you won't bring in an income and you won't be able to pay the bills, which defeats the purpose of having a business), and we address a variety of other areas such as streamlining business processes, improving confidence, managing time effectively, and reducing overwhelm.

Sagan Morrow

Chapter 2
Prioritizing Your Business

There are two important pieces to keep in mind when it comes to prioritizing your business and time management in general.

First, what we prioritize with our time management is a choice.

When we say, "I'm too busy to do XYZ," what we're *really* saying is "I've chosen to prioritize something else right now."

And the key word in that phrase? It's not "prioritize." It's actually "choice."

Whether you've made the conscious or subconscious choice to prioritize one thing over another, you are in charge of your own life. You get to control what you choose to prioritize.

With that in mind, if you're thinking to yourself that you're too busy to do something—for example, you think you're too busy to work on your business—then I want you to ask yourself *why* it is that you've chosen other things over your business, and why you aren't making your business a priority, and if you are satisfied with that choice at this stage in your life.

I want to stress here that it's absolutely okay to prioritize other things over your business sometimes. There's no need to neglect everything else in life. If you're serious about your business, however, then at some point, it does need to be a top priority... but that doesn't mean it needs to be *the* top priority every single day of every single week. Give yourself permission to take care of yourself.

The important thing isn't *what* you're prioritizing, either. It's about being *aware* of what you're prioritizing, and why you are doing that. When you pay attention to your priorities, you'll be in a better position to be intentional about every choice you make.

Ultimately, we all have the choice to prioritize one thing over another. Make sure you're aware of the choices you make so that you are an active participant in those choices and in your own life!

The second thing to keep in mind when it comes to prioritizing your business and time management in general is this: Although we technically all have the same number of hours in the day, privilege is a huge factor that comes into play.

Those of us with more privilege in life are simply going to have an easier time *managing* our time. I do not want to discount that at all. How much "choice" we have in the matter is going to differ from one person to the next, in terms of how high the stakes are in the choices we make.

Depending on your life circumstances, some of these daily action steps may be more feasible than others for you to implement. There could be many different reasons for that, and access to support systems may vary drastically depending on your geographic location, but you may find useful aid at your local women's resource centre or business resource centre.

With that in mind, I think we're ready to dive into the monthly challenges.

Grab your complimentary fillable checklists (there's one for every single chapter!) at *SaganMorrow.com/beginbook,* and let's get started...

Chapter 3

Goal-Setting & Big-Picture Business Planning

Since this is the very first month of our Begin Your Biz book, I encourage you to set a goal for yourself for the next four weeks. What do you want to accomplish by the end of the month? It doesn't matter how big or small it is, but choose a goal so you can measure your progress when we do our check-in later on this month.

Get the fillable checklist at **SaganMorrow.com/beginbook**

Day 1: What do you find most challenging about goal-setting for your business?

If you haven't set goals before for your business, or if you've struggled with it in the past, what's been the most difficult part of it for you? Write that down. (Grab the free goal planning workbook at SaganMorrow.com/workbook, which will walk you through some of the questions this month.)

Day 2: Taking "real-life" factors out of the equation (time, adult responsibilities, etc.), if you could be *anywhere* and do *anything* six months from now, what would that look like?

Dream big here! Forget about what's realistic. What's the first thing that pops into your head when you think about what you would love to have from your life and business?

Day 3: Why did you decide to be a business owner in the first place?

Understanding why you will/have become a solopreneur is fundamental to figuring out what your goals are. If you aren't aware of what it is that appeals to you the most about being your own business owner, you will struggle to come up with goals that align with your values and passions. And if you don't choose goals that are the right fit for you, then you won't put in the effort to make those goals a reality. So, consider, what are the driving factors for you?

Day 4: What do you love best about being a small business owner?

This answer might be different than you expected, and it might have changed over time. Write down your favourite thing in that workbook you downloaded on Day 1.

Day 5: What professional education can help you out as a business owner?

Here is where we ground our goals in the real world. We're balancing dreaming big with our current skill sets. What kind of professional education/experience do you have that will be beneficial to your business?

Day 6: What personality traits can help you out with your business?

What are some of your personal strengths that you can make advantageous use of as you grow your business? Write down your strengths in the goal planning workbook.

Day 7: What is your ongoing motivation for having your own business?

This may or may not align with why you started your business or with what you love best about being a business owner. For example, to break down my own experience in very simple terms, I started my own business because I wanted to do the work I enjoy best. What I love best about my business is being able to do work on my own terms. And my ongoing motivation for being a business owner is knowing that I can make a difference for other people.

Day 8: What do you see for your personal life, 10 years into the future?

The great thing about looking 10 years into the future is that it's a long enough span of time that just about anything can happen between now and then. So think about what you *really* want from life, and write it down in your workbook. Keep in mind that even if you've answered this question (or the others) about yourself in the past, I want you to check in with yourself and answer them again! We change. Life circumstances change.

Our businesses change. What was true for you three months ago might be different now. That's okay! In fact, that's great—it means you're growing and getting closer to what you want.

Day 9: What do you see for your personal life, five years into the future?

A lot can still happen in five years—but it's a little more immediate and perhaps easier to envision than 10 years! Write down your five-year personal goals in your workbook. The reason why it's so important to take your personal goals into consideration when you're doing your business planning is that you want them to work in harmony with one another. If your personal goals and business goals don't play nice together, you're going to struggle to have real success and you probably won't be very happy, either.

Day 10: Ask a friend, spouse, or colleague to help you out if you're having a tough time answering any of these questions.

It's amazing what can come out of sitting down and having a cup of coffee with someone who genuinely cares about you and your business. Sometimes even talking through your own ideas can help you uncover things you didn't expect.

Day 11: Catch up on tasks.

Are you finding the answers to these questions are coming fairly easily to you, or is there anything you've been struggling with? Take some time today to address any of the questions you had a tough time answering so far.

Day 12: How do you feel about your business life and personal life intersecting?

There's a great deal of value in connecting your business life and personal life together, especially when you are a solopreneur and you *are* your business. However, if you have misgivings about it, or if you want to create more strict boundaries between your business life and your personal life, then that will help you with guiding your big goals—for example, if you want to be able to take lots of time away from work, then you may wish to look into more passive income streams for your business.

Day 13: Look at what you need to do in your business to achieve your lifestyle goals.

If you want to travel a lot, for example, then you might want to look at how you can create a business that enables you to take time off or work from anywhere in the world or get long-term retainer clients.

Day 14: Where do you want your business to be six months from now?

This should be based in reality: think about the amount of time you'll be spending on your business in the upcoming months, and what you can feasibly accomplish over that period of time.

Day 15: Once you've got your six-month goal, consider where you want to be one year from now.

NOTE: I usually prefer to do this method the other way around (working backwards from bigger-picture goals to more short-term goals), but it works either way. It depends on whether you can more easily see where you want to be within a shorter period of time or a longer period of time, as to whether working forwards or backwards will make more sense and come easier to you.

Day 16: Think of where you want to be THREE years from now.

Hint: if you feel stuck, you can get started by taking a look at your one-year goal and multiply it by three. It can really be that simple!

Day 17: Over the past couple weeks, we've been envisioning what we want from the future. Today, let's begin putting that plan into action. Take a look at what you want from the future, and then break it down into a much smaller chunk.

Step away from the three-year mark, and look at the three-month mark. I've worked with students to help them do everything from quitting their day jobs to achieving their income goals to getting several new retainer clients within a three-month period! A LOT can happen over the course of three months if you're strategic about it.

Day 18: Map out your three-month plan of action.

Don't worry—I've got something that can help you map out your next three months with ease. It's the Business Bootcamp, a (totally free) video training to help you put together a practical three-month plan of action. Sign up at SaganMorrow.com/bootcamp.

Day 19: Do some of the lessons inside the Business Bootcamp.

You've got 15 minutes today to watch some of the videos (each of which are just a couple minutes long), so today's the day to do some learning.

Day 20: What are the top THREE things you need to do in order to achieve your three-month goal?

For example, if you want to get one long-term retainer client within the next three months, then the three things you might need to do could include building relationships with prospects, getting hired for an initial short-term project, and then upselling to a longer-term project.

Day 21: Set mini weekly goals for yourself over the next four weeks.

These should be smaller, manageable goals that will contribute toward your "larger" three-month goal. More on exactly what that could look like is in the free Business Bootcamp you joined a couple days ago.

Day 22: Organize your task list for the next week.

What is the first mini goal that you set for yourself over the next week? What are small, manageable tasks you can do every day over the next week to achieve that goal?

Day 23: Take 15 minutes today to take a step back and look at your business.

Do you have a clear idea of what you want from your business? If you've been struggling with answering the questions this month, then that's a good sign you need to spend a little bit longer with each of them.

Day 24: Take inspiration from what others are doing in their own businesses.

This will help you see examples for what YOU could work on… and how you can transform your business even when you're on a budget or on a time-crunch. Look to your business friends, mentors, or leaders in your community and listen to their stories.

Day 25: What can you do to emulate what others have done?

Building on yesterday's action step where you paid attention to inspiring stories of other freelancers, what can you do to implement something they did in their business? Not everything that worked for one freelancer will work for the next, but it's worth trying a couple of their strategies to see how it goes in your own business. There's no sense in reinventing the wheel, after all!

Day 26: Catch up on tasks today.

Today is another catch-up day: take 15 minutes to try to complete one of the tasks you might not have accomplished yet this month. What can you get done in 15 minutes?

Day 27: Identify one of the biggest lessons you learned this month.

What resonated with you while you were working on goal-setting and big-picture business planning? What are you doing differently now compared to a month ago?

Day 28: Look back at the goals you set for yourself a month ago.

Did you follow through on the goals you set for yourself? Why or why not? No judgments, here: just be honest with yourself. Write down why you did or did not follow through on particular goals, because you'll want to be able to see if you have recurring patterns each month as to what might be coming up as a repeated obstacle.

Day 29: Plan your weekly goals for the upcoming month.

What would you like to accomplish within the next four weeks? What can you do differently this coming month to achieve your goals, compared to what you did over the past month? This is a wonderful opportunity to empower yourself and get excited about your business and goals.

Day 30: Reflect back on the past month: assess your business goals and big-picture business planning.

How did this month's Begin Your Biz Challenge go for you? Have you been able to set business goals that excite, challenge, and motivate you?

Visit *SaganMorrow.com/beginbook* to access resources related to this 30-day theme of goal-setting and big-picture business planning.

Chapter 4

Create Your Business Plan

Get the fillable checklist at SaganMorrow.com/beginbook

Day 1: Check in with yourself on how you think and feel about creating a business plan.

First things first: get over your fears about creating a business plan. Business plans can be sexy! They don't need to be full of jargon. So, how do you feel about business plans? Does your heart sink at the thought of them? Or do you enjoy putting together business plans?

Day 2: Take 15 minutes today to do a FAST business brainstorming session.

Grab a large piece of paper and a few coloured pens, set the timer, and write down everything you can possibly think of that you want from your business. Listen to your favourite upbeat songs while you're at it to keep you energized and the ideas flowing. Once you're done, you might want to compare it to the brainstorming sessions you did in the previous chapter. Has anything changed, or are you still interested in focusing on the same things?

Day 3: Outline the overview/purpose of your business.

What does your business do? This is about getting to the raw, practical pieces of your business. No flowery ideas here! How do you describe your business in a few sentences so someone else can understand exactly what your business is all about?

Day 4: Create your mission statement/vision.

This differs from yesterday's action step, because the mission statement/vision is more about what you want from your business: where do you see it going? Here's where you can think more "flowery" than yesterday. Learn exactly how to create your mission statement/vision in the free Business Bootcamp: SaganMorrow.com/bootcamp.

Day 5: Outline your values.

What values does your business hold dear? Knowing your core values can make a big difference for moving forward with confidence in your business, and deciding whether or not to work with a particular client. It can also help you decide which services to focus on (because it can be tempting to come up with so many different business ideas that it begins to feel overwhelming).

Day 6: Understand why your ideal client matters.

Before you even begin THINKING about marketing your business, you need to know WHO it is that you're marketing to. That way, you'll know how to be strategic and targeted with your marketing techniques.

Day 7: Jot down a few notes about your ideal client.

We'll get much more in-depth about this in the next chapter, but for now, brainstorm just a few overarching ideas for what your ideal client looks like.

Day 8: Set goals for your business.

We got into a lot of detail on this last month, but it's always worth revisiting! Try setting a six-month goal and three-month goal for yourself. If you're already confident in the goals you set for yourself in the previous chapter, then you can simply copy and paste that into your business plan: done and done.

Day 9: Outline your revenue streams (how you'll make money).

This is a crucial part of your business plan. How are you going to bring in an income with your business? Ideally, you'll want to have a couple different revenue streams or ideas in place for how you can theoretically make money—this will be valuable when you're testing things out.

Day 10: Choose the top three ways you'll market your business.

I highly recommend using several different ways to market your business, including a combination of online and offline marketing. Diversifying will ensure you don't put all your eggs in one basket, but limiting yourself to three major strategies will also ensure you don't feel too overwhelmed with it all. We'll get a lot more in-depth with this in Chapter 6.

Day 11: Dive a bit deeper with one of the ways you'll market your business.

Perhaps you've decided to do offline (in-person) networking. Awesome! Now would be a great time to identify which events you'll attend, what you'll do to make connections at those events and gauge the success of your participation at them, how you'll follow up with connections you make, etc. Get examples of this inside the Business Bootcamp.

Day 12: Time for a SWOT analysis: today, you're going to outline your strengths.

I don't believe in false modesty—you need to recognize and OWN your strengths if you're going to make effective use of them!

Day 13: Continue with SWOT: outline your weaknesses.

Understanding your weaknesses (and identifying ways to work with/around them) is very important. Knowing what your weaknesses are is an opportunity for you to work with those weaknesses (by transforming them into strengths), or work around those weaknesses (by focusing more on your existing strengths to compensate for current weaknesses). While I don't believe in false modesty, I *also* don't believe in lying to ourselves. You need to be honest with yourself about your weaknesses.

Day 14: Continue with SWOT: outline opportunities.

What are some opportunities you can see for your business? Make a list of as many as you can think of in the space of 15 minutes. Then, you'll be able to explore ways to make use of those opportunities.

Day 15: Continue with SWOT: outline threats.

Take 15 minutes today to observe some potential threats to your business. When you set a timer and just start writing everything that comes to mind, you might be surprised at the types of things you come across. You'll be able to work proactively against those threats once you've identified them.

Day 16: Create an internal communications plan, even if you're just one person.

For example, you might want to outline a plan for regular quarterly check-ins, how you're going to prevent ideas from getting lost, etc. Basically, how are you going to ensure you don't lose track of things within your business?

Day 17: Make a plan to do internal weekly check-ins.

Every business owner should do this. Check in with yourself on a weekly basis to review what you accomplished, what you didn't accomplish (and why), and what your plan will be for the next week. This helps you to stay on track and reduces the likelihood that you'll get too caught up in "busy work."

Day 18: Catch up on tasks today.

How are things going with your business plan? Did you get stuck on any of the daily action steps so far for this chapter? See if you can get it done today.

Day 19: Create a basic client communications strategy.

How will you communicate with clients and ensure nothing slips through the cracks? What will you do to stay on the same page with them and retain them for the long-term? Focus on the broad strokes here—just jot down some initial brainstorming ideas, because we'll get a lot further into this in Chapter 9.

Day 20: Put together a vacation/sick-day plan.

It's so easy to work 24/7 in our business. Eep. Help yourself out by putting a plan in place to make room for vacations and sick days. That way, you won't be caught by surprise when you inevitably need to take a break from your business.

Day 21: Create a business finances plan.

Outline your plan for how you'll actually make money with your business: decide what your financial goals will look like and specifically how you'll earn $X each month.

Day 22: Put together your business budget.

Don't forget to include office supplies, taxes, continuing education, etc.

Day 23: Create a daily workplan for yourself.

Feeling overwhelmed and disorganized? Create a daily schedule for yourself, just as though you were working at a 9 to 5 job all day long. This is a handy appendix to add to your business plan.

Day 24: Use your business plan as a *tool* for your business.

There's no sense in creating a business plan if you aren't going to use it! It should be a tool you refer to on a weekly (if not daily) basis. How will you ensure you actually follow through and take action on your business plan?

Day 25: Take a deep breath and remember that your business plan doesn't need to be perfect... and it's okay if your business plan changes over time.

In fact, it *should* change over time, because you and your business will continue to grow—and your business plan needs to reflect that. Think of your business plan as an organic, living, working document. It's a little less scary, now isn't it?

Day 26: Catch up on tasks today.

Today is another catch-up day: take 15 minutes to try to complete one of the tasks you might not have accomplished yet this month. What can you get done in 15 minutes?

Day 27: Identify one of the biggest lessons you learned this month.

What resonated with you while you were working on creating your business plan? What are you doing differently now compared to a month ago?

Day 28: Look back at the goals you set for yourself a month ago.

Did you follow through on the goals you set for yourself? Why or why not? No judgments, here: just be honest with yourself. Write down why you did or did not follow through on particular goals, because you'll want to be able to see if you have recurring patterns each month as to what might be coming up as a repeated obstacle.

Day 29: Plan your weekly goals for the upcoming month.

What would you like to accomplish within the next four weeks? What can you do differently this coming month to achieve your goals, compared to what you did over the past month? This is a wonderful opportunity to empower yourself and get excited about your business and goals.

Day 30: Reflect back on the past month: assess your business plan.

How did this month's Begin Your Biz Challenge go for you? Have you been able to create a business plan to steer the ship of your business?

Visit *SaganMorrow.com/beginbook* to access resources related to this 30-day theme of creating your business plan.

Chapter 5

Create an Ideal Client Profile & Prospect Directory

Get the fillable checklist at SaganMorrow.com/beginbook

Day 1: Review your business plan.

Before you identify your ideal client, we need to put together background info on your business. So today, review the type of business you have—or, if you're JUST starting out, outline the type of business you want to have. Think about whether your business will primarily be online or offline, the types of services you'd like to offer with your business, and the industry or field you'll be working in, for example. If you've been going through this book chapter by chapter, then now is the perfect time to refer back to your business plan.

Day 2: Make notes today about what your business is all about.

What is the core of your business? I encourage you to free-write this and then compare it to your business plan, to ensure that you're still on track with what you originally wanted.

Day 3: Review (or outline, if you're starting from scratch) the services you offer.

Having a strong understanding of what you do is essential to knowing who you want to serve.

Day 4: What are some of the key values/primary benefits clients get from your services?

Think about this in terms of tangible benefits (such as saving time) as well as deeper benefits (such as reducing stress).

Day 5: Brainstorm demographics that you identify with on a personal level.

What are some of the things that define you for YOU? Keep these positive; they should be things that contribute to the "you-ness" of you.

Day 6: Consider what demographics define your business.

What are some of the most important aspects of your business identity? (Psst... ideally, there will be some overlap with your personal identity!).

Day 7: What are some of your strongest personal values?

Aside from demographics, values are also crucial because they will help to guide you as you make choices in your business to work with one client over another, etc. Try to think of at least three that are most important to you. If you already did this in the previous chapter, then you can copy and paste it right here—done and done.

Day 8: Outline values that are important to your business.

Do they match up with your personal values? Why or why not? How do you feel about that? Up until now, we've been working to have a better understanding of ourselves, our services, and our business—all of which are important for having a better understanding of those people we serve (AKA our clients). Tomorrow, we'll start looking at the client side of things...

Day 9: Brainstorm as many individuals, organizations, and businesses you can think of who would benefit from your services.

These should be actual, real-life examples. However, if you're still stuck, then at the very least start fleshing out the *type* of individual/business that would most benefit from your services.

Day 10: Who have you worked with in the past?

Out of those people (they can be clients, co-workers, people you've volunteered with, etc.), who did you have a positive working relationship with?

Day 11: Review that list you made yesterday.

For the people you've had a good working relationship with in the past, what kinds of commonalities do they share with each other? What do they have in common with you?

Day 12: Assess past conflicts.

It's not all sunshine and roses in the working world! Check in with yourself: what type of people have you not enjoyed working with in the past? Keeping in mind poor working relationships and identifying any commonalities can help ensure you avoid patterns of working with toxic individuals in the future.

Day 13: Who would you most love to work with?

Make a list of real people/businesses—it doesn't matter how far-fetched your ideas seem! If you could work with anyone... who would that be? Putting this list together will help you focus in and narrow down on similar characteristics, personality styles, and business types.

Day 14: Catch up on tasks today.

Some tasks might take you a bit longer than 15 minutes. That's okay—spend time today catching up on anything you might have fallen behind on. Every step counts.

Day 15: Identify 10 potential prospects who fit with the ideal client persona you've been creating over the past couple weeks.

These should be individuals/businesses who you think you have a realistic chance of working with (hint: a good place to start is prospects with whom you've already established some kind of relationship). Put this into a spreadsheet—we'll be building on it over the next few days.

Day 16: Continue with research mode.

Gather up contact information (email addresses, social media handles, phone numbers, etc.) for the 10 prospects you identified yesterday. Add those to your spreadsheet: this is the basis for your prospect directory.

Day 17: In your potential client directory spreadsheet, make notes next to each of the 10 prospects about why your services would be a good fit for each one.

This can be even just a sentence or a few bullet points, but they should be tailored and unique to each prospect.

Day 18: What's your current relationship like with each of your 10 prospects?

Have you cultivated a relationship with any of them yet? Take 15 minutes to jot down your current relationship status with each in your spreadsheet.

Day 19: What are one to three places where each prospect on your list spends their time?

Consider in-person networking events, Facebook groups, Twitter chats, etc. Add this to your spreadsheet.

Day 20: Brainstorm ways to start and/or cultivate your relationship with each prospect.

Maybe you don't have much of a relationship with the prospects on your list just yet. That's okay! Everyone starts somewhere. Consider how you can connect with them in a real, meaningful way.

Day 21: Add another 10 people to your prospect list.

Can you identify 10 more people to add to the spreadsheet? The more you have on your list, the better.

Day 22: Gather the contact info for the next 10 people and input it into your spreadsheet.

By now, you have 20 prospects plus the means to contact them in your potential client directory. This is fantastic progress for being able to build relationships and eventually pitch the people on this list.

Day 23: Make notes for why your services are the right fit for prospects #11—20.

Just like you did on Day 17 for the first 10 prospects on your list, you're going to identify how exactly your unique business and services can benefit the next 10 prospects.

Day 24: Identify where prospects #11—20 spend their time.

You know the drill: add this to your prospect list! You might even start to notice some patterns as to where your prospects typically spend their time, now that you've got 20 of them in your database.

Day 25: Do you have a relationship with any of prospects #11—20?

If so, make note of that in your spreadsheet. If not, brainstorm one or two ways you could connect with them.

Day 26: Catch up on tasks today.

Today is another catch-up day: take 15 minutes to try to complete one of the tasks you might not have accomplished yet this month. What can you get done in 15 minutes?

Day 27: Identify one of the biggest lessons you learned this month.

What resonated with you while you were working on creating your ideal client profile and prospect directory? What are you doing differently now compared to a month ago?

Day 28: Look back at the goals you set for yourself a month ago.

Did you follow through on the goals you set for yourself? Why or why not? No judgments, here: just be honest with yourself. Write down why you did or did not follow through on particular goals, because you'll want to be able to see if you have recurring patterns each month as to what might be coming up as a repeated obstacle.

Day 29: Plan your weekly goals for the upcoming month.

What would you like to accomplish within the next four weeks? What can you do differently this coming month to achieve your goals, compared to what you did over the past month? This is a wonderful opportunity to empower yourself and get excited about your business and goals.

Day 30: Reflect back on the past month: assess your ideal client profile and prospect directory.

How did this month's Begin Your Biz Challenge go for you? Are you feeling good about who your ideal client is? Have you been able to put together the beginnings of a prospect directory?

Visit *SaganMorrow.com/beginbook* to access resources related to this 30-day theme of identifying your ideal client and creating a prospect directory.

Chapter 6

Create a Marketing Plan

Get the fillable checklist at **SaganMorrow.com/beginbook**

Day 1: Check in with yourself on how you feel about the concept of "marketing."

Do you get excited by it? Scared? Anxious? Confused? Free-write what you think and feel about marketing. Get it on paper. Include here any preconceived notions or apprehensions you might have about the concept of marketing.

Day 2: Review your existing marketing plan

(if you happen to have one or if you put a skeleton of an idea of one together as part of your business plan from Chapter 4). What do you think about your existing marketing plan? How do you feel about it? Is it something that could work well for you? Be honest! If it's not something that excites you, or if it seems to stretch you too far from your comfort zone, then that's a sign it might not be right for you.

Day 3: Set a marketing goal for yourself.

This is a great way to get interested in marketing and to do it in a way that feels good and right for where you and your business are at currently. Having something to work toward will help you stay on track. What would you like to achieve with your marketing? Write that down.

Day 4: Identify why marketing is an important priority for YOU.

This is going to be the first sentence of your marketing plan. Why is marketing crucial for your business? What will strategic marketing enable you to accomplish?

Day 5: Schedule time for marketing into your workday.

It's not going to be enough to just create a marketing plan of action for your business: you also need to implement it once it's created. Figure out now a) when you're going to start implementing your plan after it's created, and b) how much time you can realistically give to marketing on a daily/weekly basis. Maybe it's 15 minutes/week. Maybe it's 2 hours/day. Regardless, decide right now how much marketing you'll need to do (based on that business plan you created in Chapter 4), and how that will fit into your workday.

Day 6: Add your elevator pitch to your marketing plan.

You already did that in your business plan, so you can just copy and paste it today. If you're feeling like your elevator pitch needs a bit of tweaking, that's okay too. Get examples of what an elevator pitch can look like in the marketing plan template you checked out on Day 4.

Day 7: Decide which types of marketing to prioritize.

Are you more interested in social media marketing (and if so, which kinds of social media platforms will you use), in-person networking, or something else altogether? Keep in mind who your ideal client is when you're choosing which type of marketing to focus the most on. Refer back to the work you did in Chapter 5 as needed.

Day 8: Identify WHY you're choosing one type of marketing over another to prioritize.

Is it because Instagram seems easier than doing in-person networking? Is it because you already have a large following on Twitter? Keep in mind that if your ideal client doesn't use Instagram or Twitter, then your marketing efforts will go to waste there. Understanding why you're choosing one type of marketing over another can be invaluable for determining whether it's truly the right areas to focus on. If not, then you should go back to the drawing board and refocus on different marketing platforms that are a better fit.

Day 9: Write a list of potential barriers preventing clients from hiring you.

Can you think of three to five reasons why a potential client isn't hiring you? Make notes of these. Focus on what your internal beliefs are and what your gut is telling you for why you haven't been hired yet (e.g. brand design looks amateur, prices are too high, don't have enough experience in the industry, etc.).

Day 10: Brainstorm ideas for overcoming yesterday's barriers.

What can you do to help reduce those barriers you identified yesterday? In other words, how can you make it easier for clients to hire you? Add these ideas to your marketing plan.

Day 11: Do market research to determine whether your assumptions about barriers were correct.

This is a good exercise for checking how well you know your potential clients, and for looking at your business from different perspectives.

Day 12: Create a longer-term timeline for your marketing plan.

Timelines are handy for seeing your marketing plan at a glance. Consider making a longer-term timeline of about six months or one year in length: it can be a simple table with two columns, one for the month and the second column featuring one or two marketing ideas to implement that month.

Day 13: Catch up on tasks.

Today is a catch-up day! How are you doing with your daily tasks for this month's challenge? Have you fallen behind on any or gotten stuck? Now's your chance to tackle them. If you've been keeping up with your daily tasks, then skip ahead to the next task (or give yourself the day off—you do you!).

Day 14: Create a shorter-term, detailed timeline.

Based on the timeline you created a couple days ago, today you're going to expand on two months and get a bit more detailed with them. What exactly are you planning on doing with your marketing ideas over the course of the next two months? Dive into those ideas a little more.

Day 15: Break down your two-month plan into eight-week chunks.

Here, you're getting super specific about your marketing efforts on a weekly basis. This is a nice method for reducing overwhelm, because it breaks down a larger concept into something that's much more manageable.

Day 16: Brainstorm what marketing efforts you'll use.

Earlier this month, you decided which ones would be at the top of your priority list... but that doesn't mean you can't have other marketing ideas on the backburner, too. Consider making a fulsome list that includes a wide range of ideas, not necessarily all of which you'll jump on board with immediately, but which can sit in your back pocket until you're ready to use them.

Day 17: List out concrete tactics for how you could use yesterday's marketing methods.

Remember, these ideas won't have to be implemented immediately. They're simply there as a backup plan and to get more ideas flowing in your mind.

Day 18: Rearrange your list of marketing ideas in order of priority.

Now that you've come up with a big list of marketing ideas, plus a few tangible ways you can carry out those ideas, it's time to organize them in order of priority. Which ones interest you the most, will be most effective, or could have the greatest return?

Day 19: Check for gaps in your marketing plan.

Before you begin implementing your plan, are there any gaps you need to fill? Is there anything missing or anything you'd like to expand upon? Do that now. (Grab the free marketing plan template at the end of this chapter to help with this).

Day 20: Incorporate a pitching plan of action into your marketing strategy.

The difference between marketing and pitching is that marketing tends to be a little more passive, and pitching tends to be a little more active. You need to actively pitch potential clients if you want to get hired! Work a plan for pitching prospects into your marketing strategy.

Day 21: Review your new marketing strategy.

Do you need to add anything else to it? Does it need editing or tweaking? Do that today.

Day 22: Add marketing into your schedule.

There's no sense in having a marketing plan if you're not going to implement it into your workday. Figure out how much time you want to spend on marketing and incorporate it into your schedule: it should be a habit, a part of your regular routine, if you want to make progress with it.

Day 23: Begin the implementation process.

Now that you've found room in your schedule for it... it's time to make good on your plan! Spend 15 minutes today marketing yourself.

Day 24: Now that you've created a marketing plan... how do you feel about it?

Are you eager to implement it? Was it fun or scary (or both!) to take action on it yesterday? It's totally normal to feel a little nervous about marketing yourself, but hopefully you'll have ideas in your marketing strategy that you want to do. It's important for you to focus on marketing tactics that stretch your comfort zone, without taking you entirely out of it.

Day 25: Celebrate your wins.

It doesn't matter how small they are—every step counts. Give yourself a pat on the back and congratulate yourself for creating your marketing plan and beginning to implement it, even if it feels a little scary. (I'd love to hear from you! Tweet at me, @Saganlives, with the hashtag #BeginYourBiz to share what you're proud of accomplishing this month.)

Day 26: Catch up on tasks today.

Today is another catch-up day: take 15 minutes to try to complete one of the tasks you might not have accomplished yet this month. What can you get done in 15 minutes?

Day 27: Identify one of the biggest lessons you learned this month.

What resonated with you while you were working on creating your marketing plan? What are you doing differently now compared to a month ago?

Day 28: Look back at the goals you set for yourself a month ago.

Did you follow through on the goals you set for yourself? Why or why not? No judgments, here: just be honest with yourself. Write down why you did or did not follow through on particular goals, because you'll want to be able to see if you have recurring patterns each month as to what might be coming up as a repeated obstacle.

Day 29: Plan your weekly goals for the upcoming month.

What would you like to accomplish within the next four weeks? What can you do differently this coming month to achieve your goals, compared to what you did over the past month? This is a wonderful opportunity to empower yourself and get excited about your business and goals.

Day 30: Reflect back on the past month: assess your marketing plan.

How did this month's Begin Your Biz Challenge go for you? Have you been able to put together a realistic marketing plan?

Visit *SaganMorrow.com/beginbook* to access resources related to this 30-day theme of creating a marketing plan.

Chapter 7
Improve Your Website

Get the fillable checklist at SaganMorrow.com/beginbook

Day 1: Assess your existing website if you have one.

Review your website with a critical eye: check how easy it is to navigate your freelance website and what your first impressions are. Our websites as freelancers are often the first point of contact with a new prospect, so it's important that they represent us well. If you don't have a website yet, then do a little research and look at other freelancer websites: what do you like/dislike about them?

Day 2: What are two or three things you could improve with your website?

Be honest! There's always room for improvement. Where do you see glaring holes? Again, if you're struggling with this action step, try looking at someone else's website: what would you do differently? Compare that to your own, and/or make a note of this so when you create your own website, you don't make the same mistake.

Day 3: Map out the purpose of your website.

If someone asked you why you have a website, would you have a good reason to give them? Do you want your website to be an opportunity to get more clients, to showcase your portfolio, to be a resource hub for retainer clients, or something else altogether?

Day 4: Does the purpose of your website match the reality?

Compare your notes from yesterday with your existing website. Ensure that the design/layout of your site matches with the purpose of it. For example, if the purpose is to get new clients, then is your Freelancer Services page easy for a new visitor to find or do they have to go digging through your website to hunt it down? (If you don't have a website yet, then brainstorm how you will map out your site to ensure it matches with the purpose of it.)

Day 5: Assess and update the top navigation of your website.

Building on yesterday's action step, take time today to critique the menu (AKA top navigation bar) of your site. What do you want people to do/see when they visit your site? Make them more likely to do that by adjusting your navigation. Again, if you don't have a website yet, then now is your opportunity to outline that top navigation bar from scratch.

Day 6: Review your About page.

When was the last time you updated your About page? Unfortunately, this page is rarely updated by most freelancers, even though it's one of the first places a new visitor will check out. You and your business are constantly changing and growing, and it's important that your About page reflects who you are currently—not who you used to be. If you're still in the process of creating your website, then today's the day to consider what you want your About page to say about you!

Day 7: Research other people's About pages.

It's okay if you're feeling stuck with writing (or updating) your About page. Get inspiration from other freelancers, and spend some time today checking out what other people have done.

Day 8: Based on yesterday's research, what did other people do that you did/didn't like?

Use that as a guideline when you're writing and updating your own About page.

Day 9: Write down your accomplishments and credentials.

Time to be proud of yourself and do a little bragging! Make notes of your credentials (professional development, diplomas, degrees, certifications, continuing education, etc.) and accomplishments (work experience, awards, successful projects, etc.). You'll add those to your About page later.

Day 10: Make notes about what drives you.

What's the "Cole's Notes" version of your business? What is it that drives you in your business? Jot that down today (you may wish to return to your business plan at this stage to double-check you're still on the same page as you were a few months ago).

Day 11: Choose a few interesting tidbits about yourself to include on your About page.

This is the final piece of your About page. Adding a few interesting things about yourself that aren't business-related will spruce up the page and help visitors get to know you better. Just be sure not to go overboard here: a couple sentences will do.

Day 12: Do a photoshoot.

When was the last time you took photos of yourself for your business? Have you ever? These are a lot of fun and a good opportunity to show your face so visitors can get to know you better (plus, it will help to increase the chance of them liking and trusting you when they can put a face to your name). Smartphones have great resolution these days, so don't be afraid to use that if you don't have a fancy camera. Ask a friend or colleague to take the photos if you don't have the budget for a local photographer.

Day 13: Choose and edit the photos from yesterday.

There are plenty of apps like A colour Story which are handy photo editing tools, even for the amateur. Lighten the photos or crop them to your liking. You'll want to choose a few of the best photos to use at various pages on your website and on social media.

Day 14: Take all this content you've created (plus your favourite photo) and add it to your About page.

Now you can piece together all that work you've done over the past week and hit the publish button!

Day 15: Reread and edit your About page.

Make sure you haven't forgotten anything crucial (e.g. contact information and social media handles, disclaimer and copyright information, photo of yourself, etc.). There should also be a good flow or transition between the various sections of your About page.

Day 16: Catch up on tasks.

It's okay if you've struggled with a couple of the daily action steps. Take 15 minutes today to see if you can catch up with a task you might have fallen behind on so far this month.

Day 17: Review your Freelance Services page.

Just like you did with your About page earlier this month, it's time to do a review of your Services page (if you don't have one, then now's the time to jot down some ideas for what you'd want on it).

Day 18: Research other Freelance Services pages.

See if you can find at least three or four different Freelance Services pages to compare and contrast.

Day 19: What are other freelancers doing that you like or dislike with their own Services pages?

Use these as inspiration when designing your own. (You should never copy what someone else is doing—that's called plagiarism! This is about getting inspiration for your own page, and helping you to identify what is and isn't effective.)

Day 20: Write down the services that you do—and don't—offer in your freelance business.

Refer back to your business plan from Chapter 4 if needed. It's helpful to make internal notes about the services that you don't offer so that you can best describe your services and market your business more effectively.

Day 21: Is your Services page easy to understand?

It's easy to get caught up in using lots of jargon, but keep in mind that your ideal client might not understand common lingo for you (for example, if you're an editor, you'll know the difference between a copyedit and a developmental edit... but your clients might not). Review the services that you offer and ensure that the language you use is written in a way that is easy for the layperson to comprehend.

Day 22: Plan and/or review your pricing model.

Do you charge by the hour? By the project? Something else altogether?

Day 23: Update your Services page.

Time to piece all these things together and hit the publish button on your Freelance Services webpage!

Day 24: Reread and edit your Services page.

Are you missing anything from it? Examples could include prices, portfolio of your work, testimonials, etc.

Day 25: Assess the rest of your website.

After updating your site so far, take a moment to look at what you've accomplished. Are you pleased with the results? Is there anything else you'd like to work on with it?

Day 26: Catch up on tasks today.

Did you fall behind on any of this month's daily action steps? No problem. Now's your chance to catch up: take 15 minutes to try to complete one of the tasks you might not have accomplished yet this month.

Day 27: Identify one of the biggest lessons you learned this month.

What resonated with you while you were working on improving your website? What are you doing differently now compared to a month ago?

Day 28: Look back at the goals you set for yourself a month ago.

Did you follow through on the goals you set for yourself? Why or why not? No judgments, here: just be honest with yourself. Write down why you did or did not follow through on particular goals, because you'll want to be able to see if you have recurring patterns each month as to what might be coming up as a repeated obstacle.

Day 29: Plan your weekly goals for the upcoming month.

What would you like to accomplish within the next four weeks? What can you do differently this coming month to achieve your goals, compared to what you did over the past month? This is a wonderful opportunity to empower yourself and get excited about your business and goals.

Day 30: Reflect back on the past month: assess your plan for improving your website.

How did this month's Begin Your Biz Challenge go for you? Were you able to make progress with your freelance website?

Visit *SaganMorrow.com/beginbook* to access resources related to this 30-day theme of improving your website.

Chapter 8

Pitch Prospects

Get the fillable checklist at **SaganMorrow.com/beginbook**

Day 1: How do you feel about pitching to potential clients?

Before we begin actually pitching potential clients (AKA prospects), we need to address a few other things related to pitching first... and that begins with acknowledging how it makes you feel. Does pitching make you feel awkward, uncomfortable, or nervous? Or do you feel excited and energized at the idea of it? Maybe you feel totally neutral about pitching. Whatever the case, make note of your thoughts and feelings about pitching, without judgment.

Day 2: Identify your biggest obstacle related to pitching clients.

Another way to look at this is, what's been holding you back from pitching to clients? Are you struggling to figure out the best approach for pitching clients? Is fear of failure holding you back? Or do you feel like you're not quite at that stage in your business yet for pitching clients?

Day 3: Understand that there's a big difference between MARKETING and PITCHING.

Marketing your business is a passive approach: you're essentially putting information about your business out into the world, and hoping that your ideal client will come to you as a result. (Psst... you can increase the effectiveness by doing *strategic* marketing and reaching out to your ideal client.) Pitching, on the other hand, is an active approach: you're actively reaching out to specific individuals about getting hired. I recommend using a combination of marketing and pitching for best results, but it's important to recognize that there *is* a difference between them.

Day 4: Brainstorm what gets you excited or motivated when it comes to pitching clients.

Is it getting to do work you love, or working with specific clients you admire, or the financial reward, or the opportunity to grow your business, or something else altogether? Likely it's a combination of several reasons—but I encourage you to identify if there is ONE (or maybe two!) primary things that really get you excited and motivated to pitch clients.

Day 5: Determine whether you feel most comfortable doing pitches in person, online, or over the phone.

I encourage you to push the limits of your comfort zone, but in the beginning, it just makes *sense* to go with what feels more comfortable for you. If you prefer to pitch in writing compared to pitching in person, then by all means go that route. When you can identify the medium that you're most comfortable with, then you can build strategies from there, using that particular platform for pitching.

Day 6: Consider what ways you prefer being "pitched at," yourself.

I make it a policy in my business to not do anything that I wouldn't want done to me, if I were the client. I recommend you adopt a similar policy. Not only will it help you narrow down a pitching strategy, but it will also empower you to feel significantly more at ease with the actual process of pitching. With that in mind, is there any type of pitch you've particularly liked? Any kind of pitching that really irks you? Make notes of this.

Day 7: Brainstorm a few ideas for how you could potentially pitch people.

Personally, I like going the route of connecting with people, understanding what their problem is, connecting it to the service I offer, and having a conversation with them in which I can organically bring up my services. But you might prefer a different approach: perhaps you want to get straight to the point with your pitch, or perhaps you'd like to make it an even longer process. There's no "right" or "wrong" way. It's about figuring out what feels natural and *good* for you and your business and your ideal clients. Today, brainstorm some ideas for how you *could* potentially pitch people.

Day 8: Do you know who your ideal client is and what services you offer for them?

Be strategic and targeted with who you pitch to! Identify your ideal client AND know which services you offer BEFORE you start pitching. It's important to have a solid understanding of your own business. So… have you created an ideal client profile? Do you have a clear idea of the services you offer for your business? If you've skipped over previous chapters where we addressed these topics, then it's important to go back and figure that out *now*, before continuing.

Day 9: Identify WHY the people on your prospect directory are in there.

You know how we created a prospect directory in Chapter 5? Now is your opportunity to dive deeper with it, and understand what it is that compelled you to add them to your spreadsheet. Why precisely do you think these people need your services? What can you do for each of them individually? You won't be able to pitch to potential clients unless you understand exactly what it is that you're pitching to them and how you can help them.

Day 10: Repeat this to yourself over and over: getting clients is ALL about relationship building.

There's a reason why we don't just come up with a list of 10 or 20 prospects and then pitch them right away. Nope! Instead, we need to focus on building relationships with these people. Think about it: would you hire someone who contacted you out of the blue, with no context? Probably not. You want to know them a bit first! Relationships are a foundational piece for building a successful solopreneur business. Yes, this means that it can take time to get clients… but the clients you get are going to be the ones you love and who want to work with you again and again.

Day 11: Review your prospect directory and assess what you know about them (and what your current relationship is like with each).

Do they know who you are? Do they know what services you offer? Have they seen examples of your work? Have you had a conversation with them? If the answer to each of these is "yes," then you might be ready to make the pitch. If your answer to *any* of these questions is "no," then it might be a better idea to build the relationship a little further before pitching your services. Make a note of your relationship with each potential client in a separate column in your spreadsheet.

Day 12: Choose two people on your prospect list and come up with a plan for how you will pitch to them.

Are you going to sit down with them over a cup of coffee? Are you going to send an email pitch (more on that tomorrow)? What method will you use to broach the subject, and how do you plan on starting the conversation and leading the dialogue toward a pitch? Outline a brief plan for two of the people on your list today.

Day 13: Try warm-pitching clients.

The idea here is to email people who you have already met or who know of you, and who will likely have a need of your freelance service, and make them an offer they can't refuse: for example, if you are a social media manager, you could warm-call them by letting them know it was nice to meet them at XYZ event, and that you'd love to continue your conversation about social media tips over coffee. This will then allow you to share more tips with them, get to know them better, and position yourself as an expert so they'll be that much more likely to hire you. So: today's action step is to try doing an email pitch. Make this even easier when you get the Email Pitch Formula inside Pitching Clients 101: SaganMorrow.com/pitch.

Day 14: Attend a networking event.

In-person events are a great way to connect with potential clients. Find a networking event near you and commit to attending it. You never know what kind of people you'll meet or what kind of conversations you'll have... and the person you're talking to just might be in need of your exact services.

Day 15: Take a deep breath and understand that timing can be EVERYTHING when pitching.

Pitch too early in the relationship and your potential client might be turned off; pitch too late in the relationship and they might already have gone in a different direction. You can navigate the issue of timing by having real conversations with your potential clients so that they know what it is you do and so that *you* know what it is they need.

Day 16: Pitch to those two people on your spreadsheet today.

On Day 12, you chose two people from your list to pitch to, and then you had the options of doing an email pitch and attending networking events. If you haven't pitched those two people on your list yet, then do that today. You've got this!

Day 17: How did it go yesterday? Assess how you felt and how it worked for you.

Yesterday you pitched a couple people from your client directory—woohoo! So... how did it feel? Did it work out okay? Assess what worked and what didn't work. Make this process easier when you get your pitching assessment worksheet inside Pitching Clients 101 (SaganMorrow.com/pitch).

Day 18: Identify what can you do differently the next time you pitch potential clients.

Now that you've assessed your first couple of pitches, you can begin preparing for your next few pitches. What can you do differently next time to be better at pitching and improve your chance of getting hired?

Day 19: Choose three more prospects and outline a plan based on how your experience with pitching went a few days ago.

Take what you learned from your first couple of pitches and apply it when you're creating strategies for pitching the next three people on your list.

Day 20: Pitch to those three potential clients.

Today's the day: you've come up with your pitching plan... so get to it! Take a deep breath and pitch to three more clients today. You can do it. (Need extra encouragement? Tweet at me, @Saganlives, using the hashtag #BeginYourBiz so I can cheer you on.)

Day 21: Assess once more how it went.

How did your three pitches go yesterday? Assess what worked and what didn't so you can be even more prepared for the next time you pitch.

Day 22: Keep in mind that if a pitch doesn't get you the results you wanted, it's not the end of the world.

There's always something we can learn from every experience. If the person doesn't hire you, *that's okay*. Learn from the experience. Identify what you can do differently next time. For example, did you pitch too early in the relationship? Were they perhaps not quite the right fit for your services? Or did you do everything right, but it turns out that there's some reason external to you for why they aren't hiring you? Not every client will hire us, and that's okay. The more you practice pitching, the better you'll get (and the easier it will be to do again), and the more likely you'll be to get hired next time.

Day 23: Add 10 more people to your spreadsheet.

Let's grow your potential client directory. After pitching at least five people so far this month, you might realize that your ideal client is slightly different than you expected. Or, maybe you've been on the right track this whole time, which is also great. Regardless, take 15 minutes today to add 10 more people/organizations to your list.

Day 24: Come up with a plan for pitching to a few more people on your list.

Review your client directory. Can you find three people on that list of 30 who you have enough of a relationship with to pitch? If so, put together your strategy for those three people today. If not, then work on building your relationship with them.

Day 25: Pitch to three more people from your list.

Pitching time! You put together your plan of action yesterday... today you're going to implement it. You've got this, my friend. Get out there and start pitching!

Day 26: Catch up on tasks today.

Did you fall behind on any of this month's daily action steps? No problem. Now's your chance to catch up: take 15 minutes to try to complete one of the tasks you might not have accomplished yet this month.

Day 27: Identify one of the biggest lessons you learned this month.

What resonated with you while you were working on pitching prospects? What are you doing differently now compared to a month ago?

Day 28: Look back at the goals you set for yourself a month ago.

Did you follow through on the goals you set for yourself? Why or why not? No judgments, here: just be honest with yourself. Write down why you did or did not follow through on particular goals, because you'll want to be able to see if you have recurring patterns each month as to what might be coming up as a repeated obstacle.

Day 29: Plan your weekly goals for the upcoming month.

What would you like to accomplish within the next four weeks? What can you do differently this coming month to achieve your goals, compared to what you did over the past month? This is a wonderful opportunity to empower yourself and get excited about your business and goals.

Day 30: Reflect back on the past month: assess your plan for pitching prospects.

How did this month's Begin Your Biz Challenge go for you? Were you able to successfully pitch prospects? Do you have a plan in place for moving forward with the pitch for other potential clients?

Visit *SaganMorrow.com/beginbook* to access resources related to this 30-day theme of pitching prospects.

Chapter 9

Client Retention Strategies

Get the fillable checklist at SaganMorrow.com/beginbook

Day 1: Assess your current clients.

This is an important first step before we get to client retention strategies. For the first half of this month, we'll focus on assessing past and existing clients and projects you've worked on. Then, in the second half, we'll move on to specific strategies you can use for retaining clients. With that in mind, spend 15 minutes today to compile a list of all the clients you've worked with recently (over the last two to six months, for example). I recommend doing this in a spreadsheet for easier organization. Pssst... if you don't have any clients yet, that's okay! It's just a sign you need to put yourself out there and start pitching. In that case, refer back to Chapter 8.

Day 2: In the spreadsheet you created yesterday, make notes of the scope of each project you worked on.

This can just be a sentence or two each, or a couple bullet points. Outline what was involved with the project. That's going to help you get a better feel for which services of yours are the most popular selling points.

Day 3: Based on the list you compiled a couple days ago, how did those clients find out about you?

Where did you connect with them? For example, did they find you via your website, did you meet at a particular event, etc. Add this information to your spreadsheet.

Day 4: Identify why each client in your spreadsheet hired you.

What was the driving factor for it? This might be because of a recommendation from someone else, or because they had an urgent problem they needed you to solve for them, etc.

Day 5: Jot down how much you enjoyed each project you worked on over the last few months.

You can even do this on a five-point scale if you like. After all, there's no sense in trying to work with clients again if you didn't enjoy the work you were doing with them. When you know which projects you enjoyed the most, you can have a better idea of what types of projects you should pitch when reconnecting with past clients later this month.

NOTE:

If you need help with simply getting clients in the first place (and you only have a couple clients you've worked with so far), then you're going to LOVE Pitching Clients 101. We take the fear and intimidation out of pitching, so you can pitch more comfortably and with confidence… and get hired by the clients you most want to work with.

Day 6: Identify one thing that worked really well for each of the projects you've worked on.

This is a fun exercise because you might see the same things crop up again and again! That will help you learn more about your strengths as a freelancer.

Day 7: Be honest about something that *didn't* work so well on recent projects.

Add that to your spreadsheet. Do you notice any patterns? Those are areas you might need to improve upon in the future.

Day 8: Make notes of your client's reaction to your finished project.

The clients who love your work are your best assets and the most likely to want to work with you again, and/or pass your name on to someone else. Consider them your "low-hanging fruit" when we start working on client retention strategies next week.

Day 9: Why did each project end?

Often this is because the project was short-term and with a specific end date or end goal in mind. Other times, it might be because you and your client mutually agreed to go in different directions. Regardless, add this information to your spreadsheet. Again, observe whether there are any interesting patterns.

Day 10: Determine how much you enjoyed working with each client.

There's no sense in working with clients you don't like. The whole point of keeping your clients is so that you get to work with awesome people. Highlight any clients you had an especially good relationship with—those are the ones you'll want to reach out to first.

Day 11: Review the comprehensive spreadsheet you've compiled over the last couple weeks.

Which clients would you be MOST interested in working with again, and which clients do you think would be most likely to have additional work for you? Prioritize them in order of which ones you think are your best bets. You're going to work your way down this list very soon.

Day 12: Catch up on tasks.

Some tasks this month might take you a bit longer than our usual 15 minutes. That's okay—spend time today catching up on anything you might have fallen behind on.

Day 13: Today's our first day to really take ACTION on client retention strategies.

Are you ready? Let's start a little easier: reach out to a past client to check in, say hello, and ask them how that project you worked on is going. This is really about touching base and showing them that you genuinely care about their company and the work you produced for them. It's not about pitching them again—instead, it's about cultivating that relationship.

Day 14: Reconnect with a past client in order to request a testimonial.

If a client loved your work, then they'd probably be delighted to provide you with a testimonial. There is, however, a "right" and a "wrong" way to do this. It's not enough to just say, "hey, can you send me a testimonial for my website?" Nope. You need to give them direction and be specific... and make it an irresistible offer. Get swipe copy for how to submit a testimonial request inside the Keep Your Clients e-course (SaganMorrow.com/keep).

Day 15: Engage with past clients on social media.

This is a nice way to let them know you're still thinking of them, whether by following them, replying to a question they ask, or sharing their post. Spend some time reconnecting with a couple clients today.

Day 16: Visit a past client in person.

Facetime makes a huge difference for a lot of clients. With that in mind, why not stop by a past client's office to say hello in person? You never know what can come out of face to face conversations, even if you only stop in to chat for five minutes.

Day 17: Give a past client a call and set up a coffee date to catch up.

This is about cultivating your relationship with them again, not about necessarily actively pitching your services. Building relationships matters in business.

Day 18: Let's get a little more actionable with our pitching today: reconnect with a past client specifically to see if they happen to have any more work for you.

This is an area where you do *not* want to come off as desperate or pushy. There's a way to word this so they'll appreciate you reaching out to them. Get swipe copy for exactly how to do this inside Keep Your Clients (SaganMorrow.com/keep).

Day 19: Collect contact info for clients in preparation for the holiday season.

Regardless of what time of year it is when you're working on client retention strategies, why not prepare in advance? Start collecting contact info for your clients now, so that by the time the holiday season rolls around, you won't have to scramble to gather their information for sending holiday cards. The holidays are a wonderful "excuse" to reconnect with past clients when you send holiday cards.

Day 20: Send a personalized thank-you note or greeting card to a past client today.

This is a thoughtful way to reconnect with a past client and remind them about you. Just make sure that you *truly* personalize it. Sending a card that says something generic defeats the purpose of reaching out. Not sure what exactly you should send to them? Get a list of ideas (and swipe copy you can use!) in the Keep Your Clients e-course.

Day 21: Time to be active in getting repeat work again: today, upsell to a client.

This works particularly well for turning a short-term project into retainer work, for example. (And yes... there's swipe copy for this inside Keep Your Clients.)

Day 22: Connect with an existing client and suggest a new project.

Take a look at what you've been doing for them so far, and what could be used to supplement that project. Think about what else you could do for them to build on existing work or to help them with something you know they're struggling with. Work that pitch!

Day 23: Have fun today—get out there and be seen.

Identify an event where you know a past or current client will be at, and attend it yourself. Spend some time chatting with them so you can touch base and serve as a reminder about your business.

Day 24: Now that you've spent some time this month reconnecting with clients, make notes in your calendar of when you'll reach out to clients again.

You can also make notes of which strategies you'd like to try next time you reach out to them. This is something you should do on an ongoing basis to keep your clients.

Day 25: Celebrate a win!

How has this month been going for you? Have you been able to reach out to past clients? Did you have success with getting repeat client work? Give yourself a pat on the back and be proud of your accomplishments. Every step you take is a learning opportunity *and* another step forward for your business.

Day 26: Catch up on tasks today.

Did you fall behind on any of this month's daily action steps? No problem. Now's your chance to catch up: take 15 minutes to try to complete one of the tasks you might not have accomplished yet this month. What can you get done in 15 minutes?

Day 27: Identify one of the biggest lessons you learned this month.

What resonated with you while you were working on client retention strategies? What are you doing differently now compared to a month ago?

Day 28: Look back at the goals you set for yourself a month ago.

Did you follow through on the goals you set for yourself? Why or why not? No judgments, here: just be honest with yourself. Write down why you did or did not follow through on particular goals, because you'll want to be able to see if you have recurring patterns each month as to what might be coming up as a repeated obstacle.

Day 29: Plan your weekly goals for the upcoming month.

What would you like to accomplish within the next four weeks? What can you do differently this coming month to achieve your goals, compared to what you did over the past month? This is a wonderful opportunity to empower yourself and get excited about your business and goals.

Day 30: Reflect back on the past month: assess your plan for retaining clients.

How did this month's Begin Your Biz Challenge go for you? Were you able to successfully keep your clients? Do you have a plan in place for moving forward with retaining clients?

Visit *SaganMorrow.com/beginbook* to access resources related to this 30-day theme of keeping your clients.

Chapter 10

Automate & Streamline Your Business

Get the fillable checklist at SaganMorrow.com/beginbook

Day 1: Outline your list of tasks that you do on a daily and/or weekly basis.

What kinds of things do you have to always do? Write down as many as you can think of in a 15-minute time period.

Day 2: Reviewing your list from yesterday, make notes of which items could theoretically be automated.

What types of recurring tasks could perhaps be done automatically, without you needing to manually do it? Perhaps this includes sending monthly invoices, email autoresponders, social media posts, etc.

Day 3: Take another look at the list you created on Day 1.

Can any of the tasks be delegated or removed entirely? Sometimes we feel as though *every* item on our list is Very Important... but often, we don't need to do them ourselves—or they are things that we really don't need to spend time or money on at all. Be as ruthless as possible. Try to note at least two things that could be delegated and two that can be removed entirely.

Day 4: Take yet another look at that big list of tasks: are there other ways you can streamline tasks?

For example, rather than checking your inbox every five minutes throughout the day (guilty as charged!), could you only check it at specific times of day and limit the number of times you open emails? That could save you tons of time and really streamline your business.

Day 5: Another way of looking at yesterday's daily prompt is this: is there anything in your business that's unnecessarily slowing you down?

Keep in mind that just because something works for someone else, or just because something *used* to work for you, doesn't mean it's necessarily the right fit for you at this point with your business.

Day 6: Ask yourself why you feel as though there are some things you can't automate, delegate, or remove.

If you feel discomfort or fear about the idea of letting go of some tasks, you need to ask yourself WHY. Understanding the foundational piece of what's holding you back will help you to overcome that hurdle.

Day 7: Make a list of the things you could do with your time if you could automate certain tasks.

For example, investing in a social media scheduler like MeetEdgar can seem pricey... but if you consider how much time you *save* in the long-term, which could then be spent doing work that pays you (such as jobs for clients), then it's absolutely worth it. Try to calculate roughly how many hours you'd save each day/week/month, and compare that to what you could do with that amount of free time.

Day 8: Create a schedule for yourself that provides you with a more streamlined business management system.

For example, set a timer for when you're "allowed" to check your emails. Blocking time off in chunks can help you juggle things more easily! We'll get more into this in Chapter 13.

Day 9: Implement yesterday's system.

Pay attention to how it goes for you. Do you like your schedule? Does it make your life better? If not, then you might need to try something different. Play around with it to find a schedule that's right for you.

Day 10: It's never too early to plan ahead, so today, create an out-of-office plan for the holidays or your next vacation.

What days are you going to take off? What do you need to make sure you do to prepare in advance so your business continues running while you're on holiday? How can you ensure that it is clear to your clients/customers when you're on holiday? Even if you don't have any upcoming holiday hours or vacation time planned, if you outline the skeleton of how you want to handle this *now*, it'll save you from needing to sort that out when you do eventually take time off.

Day 11: If you have any upcoming planned time off, add holiday/vacation hours to your website/social media accounts.

You might also want to contact clients to let them know about your out-of-office hours (so that they don't try to get their projects to you too late to work on them!). Your clients will appreciate the advance notice, and it makes YOU look good too.

Day 12: Go back to the notes you made earlier this month about which tasks could be automated.

What specifically do you need with automations? For example, I love the feature in MeetEdgar where posts can be "recycled." Make a "wish list" of your automation needs!

Day 13: Research your automation options.

There are many different types of automation tools, depending on what it is that you want to automate (emails? Social media? Something else entirely?). Take a few minutes today to do some Googling or ask your biz besties for their automation tool suggestions, based on your unique needs.

Day 14: Catch up on tasks.

Do you want to do a little more research into automation options, or are you still trying to figure out a good schedule to streamline tasks? Take 15 minutes to do that today.

Day 15: Create a standard out-of-office email responder.

That way, when you have upcoming vacation time, you can just plug in the dates without trying to figure out the exact wording you want to use. Your future self will thank you.

Day 16: Review your out-of-office plan.

Do you have everything ready? Do you know what tasks you need to quickly wrap up before you go on holiday? Take 15 minutes to review your plan and make sure you haven't missed out on anything. Keep in mind you will also want to prepare for being out of commission if/when you need sick days, so that should be written into your plan, too.

Day 17: Choose and sign up for an automation system.

Take the leap! Which automation system was on your wishlist? It's time to take the plunge and spend a little money now to save yourself time and headaches later.

Day 18: Start filling up your automation system.

You chose what automation system you're going to use for your business yesterday, so today, start filling up that automation system with content. Set the timer for 15 minutes and see how much you can add.

Day 19: Take another 15 minutes today to continue working on filling up your automation system.

It can mean more work upfront, but it will save you tons of time and stress later on down the road.

Day 20: Keep at it with filling up your automation system.

Are you beginning to see the progress you're making?

Day 21: Do you document your processes?

This is a fantastic way to keep your business streamlined. If you do anything on a monthly or yearly basis, you should absolutely document what you're doing (or even create a checklist for yourself) so that it's easier for you to remember how to do it next time. No sense in reinventing the wheel, after all.

Day 22: Take another 15 minutes today to continue documenting your processes.

Think: client intake, financial organization, blog post promotion planning, etc.

Day 23: Review your new automation system.

How do you like it, now that you've started trying it out? Reviewing these things is very important to ensure it's the right system for you at this time.

Day 24: Celebrate your wins.

Sometimes it can feel like a lot of grunt work to fill up an automated system, but it's a fantastic set-it-and-forget-it way to do business. Keep in mind that this is enabling you to focus more on doing the tasks you love! Automating your business is a form of empowerment.

Day 25: Identify ONE thing you'd like to outsource within the next three months.

What do you need in order to be able to outsource that? For example, if you need a certain amount of money, how can you start saving for it right now? Sometimes you need to spend money to make money. Start setting aside a small amount of money each week—perhaps $5 or $20, or even more—so that by a specific date, you'll be able to afford to, for example, hire a virtual assistant to help you out, or finally buy that e-course you've been eyeing up which will help make your life easier.

Day 26: Catch up on tasks today.

Did you fall behind on any of this month's daily action steps? No problem. Now's your chance to catch up: take 15 minutes to try to complete one of the tasks you might not have accomplished yet this month. What can you get done in 15 minutes?

Day 27: Identify one of the biggest lessons you learned this month.

What resonated with you while you were working on automating and streamlining your business? What are you doing differently now compared to a month ago?

Day 28: Look back at the goals you set for yourself a month ago.

Did you follow through on the goals you set for yourself? Why or why not? No judgments, here: just be honest with yourself. Write down why you did or did not follow through on particular goals, because you'll want to be able to see if you have recurring patterns each month as to what might be coming up as a repeated obstacle.

Day 29: Plan your weekly goals for the upcoming month.

What would you like to accomplish within the next four weeks? What can you do differently this coming month to achieve your goals, compared to what you did over the past month? This is a wonderful opportunity to empower yourself and get excited about your business and goals.

Day 30: Reflect back on the past month: assess how things went with automating and streamlining your business.

How did this month's Begin Your Biz Challenge go for you? Can your business keep running without you at the helm 24/7?

Visit *SaganMorrow.com/beginbook* to access resources related to this 30-day theme of automating and streamlining your business.

Chapter 11

Confidence-Boosting Strategies

Get the fillable checklist at SaganMorrow.com/beginbook

Day 1: Assess you current confidence levels on a scale of one to five.

How confident do you feel in your business? For example, if you're a freelance writer, how confident do you feel about your writing skills? Giving voice to our feelings can be a valuable way to help overcome hurdles and confidence issues.

Day 2: Identify the top one or two areas in which you struggle with confidence.

For example, this could include communicating with clients, marketing your business, the work you produce, or something else entirely. The area you struggle with the most is what we want to focus on improving this month.

Day 3: Identify what makes you feel less-than in those particular areas you identified yesterday.

It's okay to feel insecure! But understanding what it is—whether you're comparing yourselves to others, wish you had more education in your field, or something else entirely—will help you to get past it.

Day 4: What would being more confident enable you to do?

How do you think that would change things in your business and in your life? Write that down.

Day 5: Make notes of how a lack of confidence has held you back in business.

Were there missed opportunities? Get it on paper: the more "real" that you understand your confidence issues to be, the better equipped you'll be to increase your confidence.

Day 6: Identify one thing—in life or in business—that you're really good at.

Embrace that strength and own it! There's no point in false modesty. It's important to be just as aware of our strengths as we are our weaknesses. So, what's one thing you feel awesome about? If you're really struggling with this, ask a trusted friend or colleague what they'd say you're exceptional at.

Day 7: Outline what makes you good at that one thing.

Can you identify a few key reasons for why you're so good at that thing you identified yesterday? Is it your passion, years of experience, education, or something else entirely? Write that down.

Day 8: Brainstorm ways to replicate that one thing in other areas of your business.

Now that you know part of the reason for why you're so good at that one thing, is it something you can replicate over and over again?

Day 9: Choose a confidence-boosting mantra.

Your mantra should ideally fit as closely as possible to the area in which you want to improve your confidence (which we identified at the beginning of the month). Choose something short and snappy and repeat it to yourself whenever you most need it.

Day 10: Put your mantra everywhere.

There's no point in having a confidence-boosting mantra if you don't remember to actually use it. Keep it in sight so that you don't forget about it. You might want to make it your phone screensaver, write it on a sticky note you keep on your desk, etc.

Day 11: What can you do to practice your skill?

Sometimes, increasing confidence is really about increasing our experience levels. Today, brainstorm ideas for how to improve at the skill that you need more confidence in.

Day 12: Take action on yesterday's idea.

Now that you know what you can do to improve your skill or practice it, take 15 minutes to actually *do* that.

Day 13: Catch up on tasks.

It's okay if you've been having a tough time with some of these daily prompts. Give yourself a chance to catch up on something you've been struggling with. Doesn't it feel nice to cross it off your list?

Day 14: Review and update your portfolio.

When was the last time you updated your resume, portfolio of work samples, or LinkedIn profile? Do that today. Not only is this useful for potential clients to see your work experience, but it's also a valuable reminder for *you* to see what qualifications and experience you have that you may have forgotten about.

Day 15: Put what you're proud of front and centre.

When you were updating your portfolio yesterday, did you come across anything you're particularly proud of accomplishing? Put it within view of your desk so you see it every day to remind yourself how awesome you are! Maybe that's a work sample, a client testimonial, an award or certificate, etc. Whatever it is, hang it in your office or keep it on your desk.

Day 16: Give someone else a confidence boost.

Building confidence goes both ways. Let someone else know that they're awesome or why you appreciate them. Being honest and open about when we admire other people is a great way to make us that much more receptive to receiving confidence boosters, too.

Day 17: Identify someone who you admire.

Is there anyone you look up to? Find someone who inspires you to keep moving forward and achieve your goals. (This is someone that should make you feel good and happy about your work—don't fall prey to comparisonitis!) Follow them on social media or sign up for their newsletter so you can get a regular dose of inspiration from someone you admire.

Day 18: What makes that person awesome?

There's probably some particular reason(s) for why you admire that person you identified yesterday. See if you can come up with at least three reasons for why you're inspired by them.

Day 19: Identify how you can emulate them.

Keeping in mind what it is that you find so admirable about that person...

is there a way you can replicate that quality for yourself? Or do you have a similar quality that you can strengthen within yourself?

Day 20: Check whether you've been procrastinating.

Have you been postponing working on anything due to a lack of confidence? What is it? Are you still afraid to go ahead and do it, or do you think you're ready to take a step toward working on it?

Day 21: Free-write what you're worried about.

Building on yesterday's action step, take some time today to free-write what it is that scares you in business. Write down whatever you think or feel, without censoring yourself. No judgments!

Day 22: Free-write what's the *worst* that can happen if you take action.

Free-writing can be a handy way to see whether our fears are really as bad (or as realistic) as we think… and could be helpful in realizing that the truth is, a lot more doors open when we're willing to do that thing we're afraid of.

Day 23: Take a deep breath and DO it.

You've got this! Start taking action on that thing you're scared of, today. There's no time like the present.

Day 24: Assess your mantra.

How is that confidence-boosting mantra you chose earlier this month going for you? You might be ready to update your mantra or choose a different one. Or, you might find that this one is working so well for you that you're going to keep using it for the foreseeable future.

Day 25: Tell the world something you're proud of.

You might want to share on social media something you've done, or let your friends know. The point is, you're taking some time here today to vocally acknowledge that you're awesome. When you think and speak in positive ways that affirm your abilities, it will help improve your confidence, too.

Day 26: Catch up on tasks today.

Did you fall behind on any of this month's daily action steps? No problem. Now's your chance to catch up: take 15 minutes to try to complete one of the tasks you might not have accomplished yet this month. What can you get done in 15 minutes?

Day 27: Identify one of the biggest lessons you learned this month.

What resonated with you while you were working on boosting your confidence? What are you doing differently now compared to a month ago?

Day 28: Look back at the goals you set for yourself a month ago.

Did you follow through on the goals you set for yourself? Why or why not? No judgments, here: just be honest with yourself. Write down why you did or did not follow through on particular goals, because you'll want to be able to see if you have recurring patterns each month as to what might be coming up as a repeated obstacle.

Day 29: Plan your weekly goals for the upcoming month.

What would you like to accomplish within the next four weeks? What can you do differently this coming month to achieve your goals, compared to what you did over the past month? This is a wonderful opportunity to empower yourself and get excited about your business and goals.

Day 30: Reflect back on the past month: assess how things went with boosting your confidence.

How did this month's Begin Your Biz Challenge go for you? Do you feel more confident in business?

Visit *SaganMorrow.com/beginbook* to access resources related to this 30-day theme of boosting confidence.

Chapter 12

Launch a New Product/ Service/Offer

Get the fillable checklist at SaganMorrow.com/beginbook

Day 1: Make a list of all the potential ideas you have for products, services, packages, etc. you could launch.

You're not choosing anything specifically today—you're simply listing out everything you could theoretically launch. Set the timer for 15 minutes and write down every idea you have. No idea is too big or too small; all ideas are relevant at this stage.

Day 2: Take 15 minutes today to prioritize your list from yesterday.

You might want to arrange it in order of your most to least favourite ideas, the easiest to hardest ideas to implement, and/or the least to most expensive for you to create and launch. You don't have to actually choose your idea today—simply arrange your list. This will help you to mull things over and weigh the pros and cons of each launch idea.

Day 3: Choose your product/service idea for what you'll launch.

It's important you choose something that you're excited about, or else you just won't have a very successful launch. Period.

Day 4: Write down everything you need to do to create your product/service.

When you have a bullet-point list of exactly what you need to do to create your product/service, you'll be able to have a better idea of launch prep marketing plans (which we'll focus on next week).

Day 5: Identify your ideal client/customer.

Before you begin planning out how you'll market your awesome new service/product, you need to know WHO you're marketing to. Keep in mind that this might be even more specific than the ideal client you identified in Chapter 5, since it's for such a specific offer that you're launching. Regardless, you can use the same concepts to identify your ideal client.

Day 6: Make a list of what you'll need to do to prepare for your launch.

Think of this as a brain-dump—you know how much I love those! You might be feeling as though there's lots to keep track of, so get all your thoughts and to-dos out of your head and onto paper.

Day 7: Create the skeleton of a marketing/promotions plan for your launch.

Hint: focus on word of mouth and/or email marketing, as it'll enable you to connect more directly with your target audience. Refer back to Chapter 6 for some of the marketing ideas you came up with at that point.

Day 8: Create launch goals.

Knowing what you're working toward will incentivize you to keep moving forward, and it will provide you with a way to measure your progress. Refer back to Chapter 3 if you need a refresher on goal-setting tips.

Day 9: Set your launch date.

Now that you've created goals for yourself and put together a skeleton of a marketing plan and know what you need to do to get ready, you should have an accurate idea of a realistic launch date for your awesome service/product.

Day 10: Put together your plan for word-of-mouth marketing... or for your "launch team."

Are there people you can reach out to who might want to support you? Here, you're inviting people who know, like, and trust you to help you with your marketing efforts. You could, for example, invite people on your email list to share the news with their followers. But you'll get even better results if you connect with people one-on-one. Send a personalized email to those people who you have a relationship with and invite them to spread the word.

Day 11: Set up your email marketing plan.

Will you write a special set of launch emails? Or will you do a softer sell on your email list? You don't have to actually write the emails today, but outline your plan (and even the email topics or the angle you want to take for each email).

Day 12: Where do you need to be each week leading up to the launch?

Let's say your launch date is two months from now. In that case, I want you to break down where you want to be each week over the next eight weeks. For example, perhaps you need to have a certain number of email subscribers by Week 6, or you need to have your launch team organized and ready by Week 4. Outline those target numbers or other key notes for each week leading up to your launch.

Day 13: Turn those targets into action steps.

Yesterday, you figured out what your targets are each week, so now you're going to turn those targets into action steps. Learn exactly how to create actionable tasks for each week (to reduce overwhelm and actually get stuff done) in the Business Bootcamp at SaganMorrow.com/bootcamp.

Day 14: Take a step back and check in on your original launch date.

Be honest: is it realistic? It's great to be ambitious with our plans, but it's also important to be realistic with ourselves. It's okay to alter your launch date, especially if something is taking longer than expected, for example.

Day 15: Outline anything you need to purchase, outsource, and/or delegate for your launch.

It's good to think about this now so there aren't any surprises down the line. You might want to delegate something to a virtual assistant or graphic designer, or you might need to purchase some kind of equipment to make your launch happen.

Day 16: Take a look at your usual to-do list and CUT something from it.

I know this is tough to do when *everything* seems important and urgent, but if you really want to make your launch happen (and be successful), then you're going to have to reduce the time you spend elsewhere. Your task today is to let something go, so you can make room for your launch. So... what are you going to remove from your list?

Day 17: Catch up on tasks.

Have you fallen behind on this month's activities? No problem! Today's your day to catch up on tasks. Keep plugging away—you'll get there.

Day 18: Write down everything you can think of for why anyone would want your product/service.

This will help you when you come to writing your launch copy.

Day 19: Craft your marketing message for the launch.

Yesterday's exercise is going to be made practical today, because I want you to use those ideas when putting together your launch copy (AKA your marketing message). Take 15 minutes today to draft your main marketing message: this could be kind of like your elevator pitch, or a few sentences/couple paragraphs that get to the meat of what makes your offering special.

Day 20: Consider if you'll want to use supplementary resources.

When you're marketing for your launch, you might realize that you need additional materials for marketing purposes. For example, you might want to create a video as part of your launch, or you might want to create some graphics to help it pop if you're talking about it on social media.

Day 21: Brainstorm a few ideas for how you can drum up excitement for your launch.

Could you add some kind of VIP pricing, or collaborate with someone else, or host a launch party, or have some kind of special bonus for a limited time? Choose something that you're excited to add as part of your launch!

Day 22: Take a step back and review your launch plan.

How are you feeling about it? Are you overwhelmed or excited (or a bit of both)? Does it feel realistically ambitious? As you've been working on preparing for your launch this month, new things might have cropped up which means you may need to readjust your launch plans. Don't be afraid to shift things around, add, or cut to make this launch something that really *speaks* to you.

Day 23: Are there any barriers that might get in the way of your launch?

What are you going to do to handle that? Anticipating potential obstacles *now* will enable you to brainstorm ways to deal with them so that nothing stops your launch from happening!

Day 24: Big breath, and... ANNOUNCE your launch to the world.

Announcing that you have something exciting to offer is a great way to hold yourself accountable to sticking to your launch plan. And who knows—you might even find people who want to help you out, support you, or partner with you as a result of you vocalizing your launch.

Day 25: Take a break.

Seems counterintuitive when you're in the middle of preparing to launch a big offer, right? The thing is, when you take a break and step away from a project, sometimes that can give you the exact time and space you need to get a new perspective or come up with a brilliant new idea. Getting outside for a long walk in the fresh air is something I find to be particularly beneficial, but you do you: indulge in a little self-care and take a break today.

Day 26: Catch up on tasks today.

Did you fall behind on any of this month's daily action steps? No problem. Now's your chance to catch up: take 15 minutes to try to complete one of the tasks you might not have accomplished yet this month. What can you get done in 15 minutes?

Day 27: Identify one of the biggest lessons you learned this month.

What resonated with you while you were working on launching a new offer? What are you doing differently now compared to a month ago?

Day 28: Look back at the goals you set for yourself a month ago.

Did you follow through on the goals you set for yourself? Why or why not? No judgments, here: just be honest with yourself. Write down why you did or did not follow through on particular goals, because you'll want to be able to see if you have recurring patterns each month as to what might be coming up as a repeated obstacle.

Day 29: Plan your weekly goals for the upcoming month.

What would you like to accomplish within the next four weeks? What can you do differently this coming month to achieve your goals, compared to what you did over the past month? This is a wonderful opportunity to empower yourself and get excited about your business and goals.

Day 30: Reflect back on the past month: assess how your launch went.

How did this month's Begin Your Biz Challenge go for you? Were you able to successfully launch a new product, service, or other special offer?

Visit *SaganMorrow.com/beginbook* to access resources related to this 30-day theme of launching a new offer.

Chapter 13
Manage Your Time Effectively

Get the fillable checklist at SaganMorrow.com/beginbook

Day 1: Check in with yourself on what you think/feel about time management.

Does the concept make you roll your eyes because you believe there simply aren't enough hours in the day? Do you find yourself so overwhelmed by all the tasks you have to do that time management seems entirely impossible? Write these thoughts and feelings down. No judgments, just identify your reaction to the concept of time management at this point.

Day 2: How do you feel about YOUR time management abilities right now?

Is this something you excel at, or are you constantly struggling to keep up with everything in your life? How does this compare to your brainstorm from yesterday?

Day 3: What are you prioritizing one thing over another in your life right now?

Refer back to Chapter 2 for more on this topic! Remember, being "too busy for XYZ" isn't something external that happens to you. It's a choice that you make to prioritize one thing over another. So if you've recently found yourself saying, "I just don't have time to do XYZ," then you might want to take a step back and ask yourself why you're prioritizing something else instead… and whether you're okay with the way you're currently prioritizing things.

Day 4: Identify your #1 business priority.

What is the MAIN thing you need to focus on in your business at this point with your business? Check in with your business plan when considering this.

Day 5: What are three things you need to do to get closer to your #1 business priority?

For example, if your main priority is to get more clients for your freelance business, then three things could include a) getting business cards, b) attending networking events, and c) connecting with past clients to see if they have additional work for you or colleagues who might be in need of your services.

Day 6: Identify ONE thing in your life that you can let go of or cut back on to make more room for your business priorities.

I know how hard this can be, but I bet there's at least one thing you can temporarily cut back on or reduce the amount of time you spend on it, which will free up that time to spend on your business instead.

Day 7: Identify what mindless and mindful tasks you can combine.

For example, I love listening to podcast episodes while cleaning the house. If you work from home especially, this will help you to feel like you're not missing out on something, or that you're "neglecting" your duties.

Day 8: Spend money on something that will save you time.

Recent studies suggest that when you spend money on time-savers rather than more *stuff*, it actually makes you happier. So... what can you treat yourself to that will save you time? Go on—treat yourself to something that will save you a ton of time in your business.

Day 9: Organize your tasks based on day of the week.

Take a look at the schedule of your life: are there certain commitments you need to attend to on specific days of the week? That's okay! Block off any days that you need to. Which days are you left with to work on your business? Can you specify certain days to work on certain parts of your business?

Day 10: Block off time at the beginning of every single week to outline what you'll work on over the coming week.

I find Sundays to be the perfect day of the week to do planning for the upcoming week. Try to break it down into manageable tasks: one task to accomplish every single day.

Day 11: Choose just one activity each day as your main priority.

Ignore EVERYTHING else in your business so that you can complete that one item and cross it off your list.

Day 12: Organize your tasks based on time of day.

Once you've chosen broadly what to work on each day of the week, now you can narrow it down farther. For example, choose a specific timeframe (such as from 11am to 11:30am) every single day to respond to emails.

Day 13: Automate something in your business.

Remember how on Day 8, we looked at the importance of spending money to save yourself time? Well, you might want to consider spending money on some kind of automation. For example, I love using MeetEdgar as a social scheduler to schedule posts on Twitter and Facebook ahead of time. This leaves me with more time to do other things (including connecting with people on social media in real-time!).

Day 14: Delegate something in your life to someone else.

This is going to free up time to work on your business. For example, can a spouse, child, or roommate take on extra chores around the house for the next couple weeks while you get systems in place for your business? Even getting temporary assistance can help you get back on your feet.

Day 15: Delegate something in your business to someone else.

Could you hire a virtual assistant to do something that you don't know how to do or don't like doing? Pssst... you could even do a skill-swap with someone else if you feel like you have $0 to spend.

Day 16: Delegate things that you don't know how to do, don't like doing, or will take too much time for you to do yourself.

As with anything in business, it's important to be strategic. Choosing what to delegate, who to delegate it to, and when to delegate, is no different.

Day 17: Catch up on tasks today.

How are things going for you this month? Take 15 minutes to try to complete one of the tasks you might not have accomplished yet this month. It's okay if a particular 15-minute action step is something you're struggling with—try taking another stab at it!

Day 18: Choose a system that works for you.

At various stages in my business, I've used different systems for managing tasks: colour-coded sticky notes on poster paper, Asana, Google docs, spreadsheet, dry-erase to-do list... The point is, different systems will work for you at different points in your business. Find what works for YOU, at this particular point in your life/business.

Day 19: Take 15 minutes to assess what you can copy and paste in your business.

For example, you don't necessarily need to find *new* clients—you might be able to reconnect with past clients and ask them if they have work for you. Or, you might be able to repurpose content from a blog post or email newsletter on your social media account. Get creative!

Day 20: Implement what you assessed yesterday.

Follow up with a past client or copy and paste blog post content into social media posts, for example. Recycling works just as well in business as it does with your kitchen's recycling bin!

Day 21: Set timers for what you'll be working on.

That way, you'll be able to stay on track and get stuff done within a specified timeslot.

Day 22: Celebrate a win.

What are you super proud of yourself for accomplishing so far this month? It doesn't matter how seemingly small it is—every step counts and should be celebrated. Be proud of what you've done and give yourself a pat on the back, and let someone in your life know about it so they can cheer you on, too. (If you don't feel like you have someone to support you, then Tweet at me, @Saganlives, with the hashtag #BeginYourBiz to let me know what you're proud of so I can be your cheerleader!)

Day 23: Set aside time to check in with yourself at the end of each week.

Earlier this month, we talked about doing your planning for the week at the beginning of each week... well, I also want you to do a check-in at the end of each week. Assess how things went for you this week, what you did/didn't get done, and why. That will help you identify flaws in your systems/strategies so you can adjust and keep moving forward.

Day 24: Find an accountability buddy.

Do you have someone ELSE who you can check in with on a regular basis? It could be once a week or once a month. Find a business friend or a business coach—someone who will check in with you and see how you're going, and keep you accountable to your own business. It's okay to need a little hand-holding sometimes: we *all* need that from time to time. Acknowledge that and then find someone to hold you accountable to your work.

Day 25: Give yourself permission to be human.

The reality is that sometimes, life gets busy and we need to just let things go and take a day off for self-care. And that's okay. Honour yourself when you need to take time away from work, and remember that—although your business needs to be a top priority in your life—it doesn't have to be a top priority 24/7. You can occasionally give yourself a break and get some much-needed rest from your business.

Day 26: Catch up on tasks today.

Today is another catch-up day: take 15 minutes to try to complete one of the tasks you might not have accomplished yet this month. What can you get done in 15 minutes?

Day 27: Identify one of the biggest lessons you learned this month.

What resonated with you while you were working on improving your time management abilities? What are you doing differently now compared to a month ago? How have your thought processes shifted around the concept of time management?

Day 28: Look back at the goals you set for yourself a month ago.

Did you follow through on the goals you set for yourself? Why or why not? No judgments, here: just be honest with yourself. Write down why you did or did not follow through on particular goals, because you'll want to be able to see if you have recurring patterns each month as to what might be coming up as a repeated obstacle.

Day 29: Plan your weekly goals for the upcoming month.

What would you like to accomplish within the next four weeks? What can you do differently this coming month to achieve your goals, compared to what you did over the past month? This is a wonderful opportunity to empower yourself and get excited about your business and goals.

Day 30: Reflect back on the past month: assess your time management abilities.

How did this month's Begin Your Biz Challenge go for you? Have your time management abilities improved? Even the smallest change can have a ripple effect!

Visit *SaganMorrow.com/beginbook* to access resources related to this 30-day theme of improving time management.

Chapter 14

Reduce Overwhelm in Business

Get the fillable checklist at SaganMorrow.com/beginbook

Day 1: Identify what you feel most overwhelmed with in your business right now.

I know it's tempting to say "everything!", but I bet there are a few crucial things that make you feel more overwhelmed than others. Is it trying to figure out what direction you should take your business in? Managing clients? Marketing your business effectively? Write that down.

Day 2: Do a brain-dump of all your thoughts and business ideas.

This is one of my favourite ways to beat the overwhelm. Get all those thoughts and ideas spinning around in your mind on paper, so that it's out of your head.

Day 3: Organize your ideas based on similarity (group them together where possible).

Once you get all your ideas written down from yesterday's brainstorm, then you can organize them into lists, or perhaps draw colour-coded circles around similar/grouped items. This will help you to see where there's some overlap and get a clearer picture of how to organize it all better. For example, maybe you have ideas around starting a variety of different kinds of services, or perhaps you want to write a book, or maybe you want to explore new marketing methods.

Day 4: If you're trying to decide what ideas you should focus on with your business, then take notes beside each of your ideas/thoughts based on a) your interest level, b) your skill

level, c) the time/monetary commitment, and d) the return on that item.

Once you do this, you might start to see which areas you can prioritize, and you might notice that some of your efforts haven't been put in the most beneficial parts of your business.

Day 5: If you're stuck on what you should choose to prioritize, go with the idea you're most interested in.

You can improve your skill. You can find time or money for your idea. But passion and interest in your idea is something you absolutely, fundamentally, need to have in order for you to give it your all and have success with it.

Day 6: Do a brain-dump of all the tasks and priorities you have right now for your business.

This could include things like a list of all your clients, behind-the-scenes administration tasks, etc.

Day 7: Once again, organize your brain-dump of tasks into groups.

Do you have a lot more tasks listed under one area compared to another? Is your client area looking a little slim, for example? Organizing your tasks into grouped areas will enable you to see what you need to make more of a priority for in your business.

Day 8: Assign a rough time estimate per week to each of the tasks you listed yesterday.

For example, if you have a client on retainer, mark down how many hours you need to do work for them on average on a weekly basis.

Day 9: Once you have average time estimates on a weekly (or monthly) basis for your tasks, which we did yesterday, then you can start looking at which items you can cut back on in your business.

Is anything taking up way more time than it should? Or does it turn out that you actually have a lot more time than you expected in your day?

Day 10: Do a brain-dump of all the questions you have about your business.

Can you tell I like brain-dumping? But seriously, this is a really useful stage to go through. What kind of questions do you have about business? List as many as you can think of in the course of 15 minutes.

Day 11: Identify where you can go to get the answers to your questions.

Is there an expert you can consult? A book you can read? A course you can enroll in? Research you can do on your own? Decide what you plan to do to learn the answers to your business questions.

Day 12: Take the time to breathe deeply and slowly.

The science behind the correlation between breathing and feeling more relaxed is super cool, and even better, it really doesn't take that much time or effort out of the day. The trick is to be conscious about breathing. Today, practice breathing so that when you feel stressed, it'll be easier to do it.

Day 13: Ask yourself what you want out of your business in the next five years.

Here's the thing: you can't exactly identify the best things for you to be working on NOW, if you don't know where you want to GET to. That's why it's so important to do some bigger-picture planning for your business. The next few days ask you questions similar to what we looked at back in Chapter 3 because they're worth revisiting at this stage of your business.

Day 14: Ask yourself what you want out of your life in the next five years.

Do you want to move to a different city, or start a family, for example? Asking yourself what you want from your life is fundamental to your home business goals, as you'll see tomorrow. Write down one thing you want from your life in the next five years.

Day 15: Take a look at your action steps from the previous couple days: do your business and life goals match up? (Hint: they should!)

If your business and life goals mesh well together, then that's a good sign that you're moving in the right direction with your business idea. If not... then you might want to rethink things a little.

Day 16: Set a goal for yourself, one year from now.

It could be a goal to make $X with your business, to have X number of clients, to quit your day job... anything goes! Refer back to Chapter 3 if you want a refresher on setting goals.

Day 17: Where do you need to be, six months from now, in order to reach your one-year goal?

This is your ticket to making life a little easier. Looking ahead to the future will help you to identify the best action steps to take NOW.

Day 18: Where do you need to be, three months from now, in order to be where you need to be in six months?

Now that you know (from yesterday) where you need to be six months from now, in order to meet your one-year goal... it's time to figure out where you need to be three months from now, in order to meet your six-month goal. Why do we do this? Because breaking down your larger goals into more manageable ones can be a game-changer for taking action. So... where do *you* need to be three months from now?

Day 19: Check that your small daily goals contribute toward your big-picture goals.

There's a big difference between big-picture goals and smaller daily goals, and you need to have a balance of the two for any business! There needs to be alignment between them, or else what are you working toward? Make sure the smaller tasks you work on contribute towards your larger goals. Is there any disparity between your smaller goals and your larger goals? If so, do something about it: make a change to your business structure so that it's streamlined.

Day 20: What is ONE thing you can do with your business TODAY to take a step closer to where you want to be in the next three months?

Do it right now. Look at you! You're now that much closer to achieving your goals.

Day 21: Take a look at your weekly time-sucks: where does your time and energy go each week?

Are you satisfied with where all of it goes? Is there a change you could make? For example, if you get caught in the "Instagram loop," as I like to call it (I can't stop scrolling until I've seen all the new content!), then reserve only looking at Instagram when you're waiting for the kettle to boil or when you need a break from work, for example.

Day 22: Identify one thing in your life that you can eliminate in order to make room for business items.

Remember, even 15 minutes here and there can make a big difference. Do some brainstorming—you might discover that you can make more time for your business than expected.

Day 23: Above all, when it comes to reducing overwhelm, you need to ask yourself one simple question: "Am I being honest with myself about what I *really* want and what my obstacles are?"

If you find yourself giving excuses for why you haven't done XYZ, it might be time to take a good hard look at your options. It might be that you need to put something on hold in your life or to spend a little bit of money now in order to achieve your goals—but I bet that if you take a good hard look, there will be something you can do to keep making progress with your business and go further in the direction that fires you up.

Day 24: Honour where you're at.

It's important to be honest with yourself about what's going on, but that doesn't mean you should beat yourself up over it! Every single choice you make, every single step you take, is what gets you to overcoming the overwhelm and achieving your goals. You've got this.

Day 25: Find a business bestie to chat, support, and commiserate with.

You don't have to go it alone. What could a business bestie help you with? You might want someone to help you keep accountable, brainstorm ideas with, or share your struggles and wins with, etc. Having someone else around to help you out and support you can make all the difference for reducing overwhelm!

Day 26: Catch up on tasks today.

Today is another catch-up day: take 15 minutes to try to complete one of the tasks you might not have accomplished yet this month. What can you get done in 15 minutes?

Day 27: Identify one of the biggest lessons you learned this month.

What resonated with you while you were working on reducing overwhelm? What are you doing differently now compared to a month ago?

Day 28: Look back at the goals you set for yourself a month ago.

Did you follow through on the goals you set for yourself? Why or why not? No judgments, here: just be honest with yourself. Write down why you did or did not follow through on particular goals, because you'll want to be able to see if you have recurring patterns each month as to what might be coming up as a repeated obstacle.

Day 29: Plan your weekly goals for the upcoming month.

What would you like to accomplish within the next four weeks? What can you do differently this coming month to achieve your goals, compared to what you did over the past month? This is a wonderful opportunity to empower yourself and get excited about your business and goals.

Day 30: Reflect back on the past month: assess your feelings of overwhelm.

How did this month's Begin Your Biz Challenge go for you? Have you been able to reduce overwhelm in your life/business?

Visit *SaganMorrow.com/beginbook* to access resources related to this 30-day theme of reducing overwhelm in business.

Chapter 15

Next Steps

Perhaps you devoured this book very quickly, or maybe you decided to go through it day by day and you've therefore been reading it over the course of an entire year.

Regardless, you might at this point be wondering... *Where do I go from here?*

At some point you'll need to set aside more than 15 minutes in a day to work on your business. But when you're strategic and intentional about what you spend your time and energy on, you'll be able to empower yourself to *save* a lot of time and energy. And hopefully, by reading this book, you'll have gathered the tips and skills needed in order to begin doing that.

You might, in fact, discover that you already know the answer of what the next step is for your unique situation.

Every person and business is different. Keep moving forward. Keep using your business plan to steer the ship of your business (and remember that you can change it as much and as often as you like: you're the captain of the ship, after all!).

I encourage you as well to take a look at the notes you made on Day 28 of each month over the past year: were you able to accomplish the mini monthly goals you set for yourself or not? If you weren't able to, then do you see any particular reasons for this, or patterns as to the obstacles you faced? Recognizing patterns when we struggle is useful because it can enable us to come up with solutions to change those patterns.

As a general rule, the trick with business is to have a goal in mind, some kind of destination you'll be pausing at before travelling to the next goal (and the next... and the next...), while still paying attention to what's going on in your immediate vicinity. What you do today should in some way contribute to your larger plan, your bigger goals. And when you look at it that way, it will be easier to see what next steps make the most sense for you to take as you move forward and build your awesome freelance business.

You've made a lot of progress with your business by following along with each of the daily action steps in this book! It doesn't matter how fast or slow you go: progress is still progress. Everyone's journey is different. Be proud of all that you have done, celebrate your wins, and know that you have what it takes to persevere.

Chapter 16
Additional Resources

Want a little help along the way with your freelancing journey? This chapter includes all the resources you need!

Grab (free!) fillable checklists for each of the chapters to make it easier than ever to keep track of each of the daily 15-minute action steps: **SaganMorrow.com/beginbook**

Also at SaganMorrow.com/beginbook, access links to all of the resources mentioned below:

Blog posts:

- Inspirational stories: what two freelancers did to start & grow their businesses

- Identifying your ideal client: step-by-step guide

- How to build a prospect list

- Marketing strategy template

- How to get retainer clients: step-by-step marketing plan

- How to write an About page

- How should you set rates as a freelancer?

- 10 things to include on your Freelance Services page

- How to grow your small business without a team

- 20+ confidence-boosting mantras

- What you need to know when preparing for a launch

- Accountability tips for freelancers
- Dry-erase to-do list
- Business planning tips for solopreneurs
- Difference between a business best friend and a business coach

E-courses:
- Pitching Clients 101
- Keep Your Clients
- Monetize Your Blog With Freelance Writing
- Goodbye 9 to 5

Software:
- Toggl (time tracking)
- Zoho (bookkeeping)
- MeetEdgar (social media scheduler)

Join a community of hundreds of other new freelancers inside the Begin Your Biz Facebook group at *SaganMorrow.com/begin*

About the Author

Sagan Morrow has over a decade of experience as a blogger and freelancer across a variety of industries. She is the author of *The Business of Writing & Editing: Practical Tips & Templates for New Freelancers*, and she also teaches online courses to empower new freelancers as they grow their own successful, profitable businesses.

Sagan has a degree in Rhetoric, Writing & Communications and is based in Winnipeg, Canada. In addition to her work with other freelancers, she also writes polyamorous romance novels. Learn more about Sagan and access free resources for freelancers at SaganMorrow.com.

Connect with Sagan on Twitter and Instagram: @Saganlives

www.ingramcontent.com/pod-product-compliance
Lightning Source LLC
Chambersburg PA
CBHW020559220526
45463CB00006B/2366